CORNISH
FAMILY NAMES

Cornish
Family Names

Bob Richards

First published 2009

The History Press
The Mill, Brimscombe Port
Stroud, Gloucestershire, GL5 2QG
www.thehistorypress.co.uk

British Library Cataloguing in Publication Data.
A catalogue record for this book is available from the British Library.

ISBN 978 0 7524 4976 0

Typesetting and origination by The History Press
Printed in Great Britain

CONTENTS

INTRODUCTION

Have you ever thought about the meaning and origin of your surname or family name? We all have them, some we even share with others to whom, as far as we know, we are not related. So how did we come to share a common name?

Was there a time when all of us with the same surname were related? Who was it that first gave us that name, and why? How common is your surname? Do you share it with anyone famous in history?

These are some of the most common questions I am asked about the origins of names and what follows is an attempt to seek out the origins and frequency of some names commonly found in Cornwall. But where to begin? That was the big question.

In reaching the answer to this, I looked at Cornwall's history. Today it is, like most places, a mix of folk whose families have lived here for many generations and folk who, for a variety of reasons have come here to live in more recent times. People come here today to work from places far and wide. Many people come here to retire, having perhaps enjoyed their family holidays here for many years when younger. So to take the most common and popular names today in Cornwall would perhaps not do justice to some which have been around for centuries, and so I have looked back almost 150 years to the census of 1861.

Census records of one sort or another have been around ever since people began to gather information about their fellow citizens. Governments across centuries have wanted to gather information for purposes of taxation and mustering armies and so on, but the census as we know it today is relatively new. The first real attempt at a modern type of census was in 1801, but this was mainly just a head-count of the population with no full details of age, occupation or where they were born. The first census as we would recognise it was taken in 1841, but even this has its limitations, particularly in age and place of birth of the population. With gradual improvement in the amount and accuracy of the information gathered and with the exception of 1941 when the Second World War intervened, the census has taken place once a decade ever since then. Looking at information gathered from these census records, I found that the population of Cornwall peaked in the 1861 census. It had almost doubled from around 188,000 in 1801 to over 369,000 in 1861. It then began dropping off until by the census of 1901, Cornwall's population was down by over 50,000 on its 1861 peak.

I don't want to dwell too much on the reasons for this, they are the subject of many volumes down the years, and most of them relate to the severe downturn in the fortunes of Cornwall's tin and copper mining industries.

1861 was also just before the era of mass transport. Railway links between many of Cornwall's mines and its coastal ports had been in operation for a generation or more, some horse-drawn, some drawn by the newly invented steam engine, but the era of mass travel by rail was just around the corner. Within a couple of decades, Cornwall had the beginnings of its tourist industry. More folk were moving further perhaps than they ever had before at any time in history, whether it was looking for work or, for those who could afford it, exploring parts of the country they had never visited before.

For a variety of reasons then, the demographic profile of the population of Cornwall after the 1860s changed forever. So where better to begin?

As with a study of most subjects, it is possible to say 'this has been done before', and so it is with studies of surnames here in Cornwall.

Indeed one name on the 1861 census seems to have been the first to have a go at such a work. He was John Bannister. Described on that census as 'Perpetual Curate of St Day', he was born in York in 1815 and married a lady from Belper in Derbyshire. He moved to Cornwall only in his mid-forties. He died here in 1873 at the age of fifty-eight so what, you may ask, were his qualifications to write such a work on Cornish names? Possibly none other than curiosity and a desire for knowledge of his flock and those around him.

Others have looked at the subject down the years and one such study was by another man from St Day, Richard R. Blewett, who was schoolmaster there for many years. He took over three years to study the 1953 Electoral Register of Cornwall, analysing it and dissecting it in minute detail, later publishing his findings over a series of articles in *The West Briton*. His research also took in the correlation between surnames and place names, one which is quite apparent in many family names and which I will touch on many times in this book. There are many works on family names and place names in addition to those already mentioned.

But why do we have family names at all? Put in its simplest form, if you were known as Peter, way back in the mists of time, possibly even before the Norman Conquest, then everyone knew who you were, until someone else named their child Peter in the same settlement. Then it was possible to become confused if anyone asked for Peter. Which one? Was it the one who lived down by the stream or the one who lived on the nearby hill?

To distinguish, you may have added a second, or surname, to Peter. Using the language of the time, the Cornish Celtic language, Peter who lived near the stream would, over time, become Peter *Dowr*, or Dower as we more commonly see it today, and Peter who lived on the hill would become Peter *Brea*, or Bray as we now more commonly see it. These would be derived from *Dowr*, meaning 'stream' or 'river', and *Brea,* meaning 'hill'.

This is very simplified and without question these names took generations to come into common use, but thereafter you named your children with your family or surname and so we still have them, down to modern times.

Occupations could also give you your name; Miller, Thatcher, Carpenter and so on have all derived from men who followed those occupations in their daily lives.

Place names can also derive from the names of folk who lived there. In his introduction to his first *West Briton* article, Richard R. Blewett says:

There was a man whose name was Lywci and he was a Celtic slave in bondage to a Saxon lord. Before this lord died the fear of the fires of the hereafter smote him and 'for his soul' he was freed upon the altar of St Petrock, Bodmin. Heaven would be sure to see that, but to make doubly sure, Lywci's name was written on the blank leaves of the Bodmin Gospels…I like to think that they gave Lywci a piece of land and called it Lwyci's farm or Trelwyci. By 1298 it was spelt Trylouky. It is spelt Trelucky today and is in the parish of Cuby. In 1953, thirteen adults were left in Cornwall named Lukey or Lukies. A witness to the manumission of Lywci was a Celtic Mass Priest called Bryshi, who might have changed his job and become a farmer on Bryshi's Farm or Trebryshi; by 1199 it was spelt Trebursi, today it is Trebursye in the parish of South Petherwin. In 1953 there were twenty nine adults in Cornwall named Bursey. There's romance for you in two Celtic Cornish surnames.

The *Bodmin Manumissions*, or *Bodmin Gospels*, the freeing of slaves upon the altar of St Petrock's, Bodmin, are an exceptional survival from about the tenth century and well worth lengthier study than space allows for here. Suffice to say that for purposes of this work, well over a thousand years later, they give a reference point, and one which I am happy to acknowledge was brought to my attention by the writings of Mr Blewett some fifty years and more ago.

Romance aside, how do we go about choosing a list of names for a book like this? The 1861 census is a useful start point for the reasons explained but here we find that the five most common surnames in Cornwall are Williams, Thomas, Richards, Rowe and Harris in that order, each with over 3,000 entries. So why not begin there?

Simply because they are not exclusive to Cornwall or even verging on having the majority of their bearers from this county. The names I have selected are either exclusive to (or very nearly exclusive to) Cornwall, or have excellent credentials for being considered Cornish by the majority of the folk who have them. The name of Combellack, for example, appears just over a hundred times on the 1861 Cornwall census, but there is only one other holder of that name in England on the same census. The name of Chegwin, including its variants of Chegwen and Chegwyn, has over 100 of its 111 nationwide holders here in Cornwall with one of the absentees being a sailor, born in Cornwall and living in Portsmouth, and one 'stray' family bearing the name in the Liverpool area. These, although less common in pure terms of numbers, are far more Cornish, dare I say, than Williams or even my own name of Richards. Furthermore, although many Cornish bearers of the name of Williams can track their Cornishness back many generations, and indeed my own Cornishness in the Richards line can be reliably traced back as far as St Just in Roseland parish registers permit, to the year 1610, I have omitted these names in favour of those which can claim some form of uniqueness to Cornwall, or certainly a majority of their bearers from this part of the world. It is also of interest to note that many names occur right across the county from the Penzance district to the Tamar but some, despite proven origins

St Michael's Mount, a place associated with many of Cornwall's leading families down the centuries.

many centuries old, have stayed in one small corner of the county in a few adjacent parishes. There seems to be no consensus for why this should be but I would offer the following as one likely explanation, particularly for those in the far west of Cornwall. It comes from the preface to the book *Hearthside Stories of West Cornwall,* first published in 1870. Its writer, William Bottrell, we shall meet later, but he offers the following:

Before the commencement of the present century, the district of West Penwith…was, from its almost insular position, one of the most secluded and unknown parts of England. The estuary of Hayle, by which it is bounded in the east and the Mount's Bay approaching within three miles of each other, sever it in some measure from the rest of the county, with which, some three score years ago, from the badness of the roads and scarcity of wheel-conveyances, it had but little communication, either commercially or otherwise. Then, persons living west of Penzance, were regarded as great travellers if they had 'crossed the Hayle', which at the time was a dangerous undertaking on account of its shifting quicksands, and people living further east were looked on as foreigners by the west-country folk. Indeed, few persons can form an adequate idea of the singular seclusion in which the inhabitants of West Penwith existed.

We probably do not give the remoteness of West Penwith a second thought as we zoom down the A30 these days, but only a century or so ago it was a long way from anywhere. As we shall see, many of the names whose geographical spread is very limited are indeed from this West Penwith area. Perhaps Mr Bottrell has a point here.

In addition to pure numbers and meaning, it has also been of interest to find holders of many of these Cornish names who have achieved some kind of fame or even notoriety, either here in their native county, or in the farthest corners of the world. Therefore apart from a few lessons in where the names may have originated, what follows is also a look at some of those who have borne the name with a degree of distinction and honour down the years in a huge variety of walks of life, from war heroes and explorers through to priests, missionaries, authors and a host of others.

The achievement of fame or notoriety has, however, not been a deciding factor in whether to include or exclude any particular name, and the exclusion of a short biography from any particular name is certainly not an indication that no bearer of the name has ever achieved anything of note. Finding one for each name was not the plan. They are included merely to add to the reader's general knowledge and understanding of this race of folk we call Cornish, and to note some of their contributions to the world of their generation.

To return for a moment to Mr Blewett's work of the 1950s, he says in a letter accompanying his *West Briton* articles, 'In a study of this nature, to err sometimes is inescapable and even the most learned in the Celtic Cornish language will not agree on the correction of the errors.'

So, here goes, not being 'the most learned in the Celtic Cornish language' I hope that I have come to conclusions, with the help of others whose studies I have referred to, which will be acceptable. Often there is a difference of opinion on origins, and where this occurs I have noted those I have found and tried to be fair in giving a choice. I have not tried to be judgemental or even critical without evidence or strong information to detract from an apparent origin.

To err is human and as Mr Blewett says, is inescapable.

CORNISH FAMILY NAMES

ANDREWARTHA

The name contains three elements, *an dre wartha*, all of which can be directly related back to the Cornish Celtic tongue. The *wartha* element refers to high ground and the *dre* or *tre* is a homestead or farm settlement, so we have the folk who live on the farmstead on high ground. The name also appears as Trewartha, with the same early meaning. There is a Trewortha Farm and Trewortha Tor, as it is spelt on modern maps, on Bodmin Moor in the parish of North Hill. Both lie at around 300 metres above sea level, almost as high as you can get in Cornwall, providing ample justification for the name. It is an area steeped in history. Close by we find The Hurlers, Stow's Pound and a host of other antiquities clearly indicating human settlement for many millennia. At Trewortha Farm, three Bronze Age round houses have been constructed in recent years in as authentic a manner as possible to act as an educational aid to modern generations exploring the area. Evidence of human habitation from the Bronze Age is abundant with cairns, cysts and field systems all to be found here. Further evidence of more modern habitation is also found in well-preserved medieval landscaping and field systems.

On the name itself, the census of 1861 shows just over 150 Andrewartha or Andrawartha names, well over half of which are concentrated in the Helston and Penzance districts in the west of the county. The parishes of Germoe, Perranuthnoe and St Hilary each have concentrations of the name, and mining is the main occupation of these families.

Of the almost 100 Trewartha names, over half are to be found in the Redruth registration district, particularly concentrated around the parish of Gwennap where again mining is the main occupation.

Among those bearing the name today are Australian actress and former *Neighbours* star, Janet Andrewartha. She played the part of Lyn Scully in the Australian television series from 1999 to 2006.

A quick look at the Cornish Quarter Sessions records shows that not all those who have borne the name over the years have been of impeccable character. Take the example of Ann Andrewartha of Breage, who was convicted in 1830 of stealing ten yards of calico, two bed sheets and pillow cases belonging to one William Baker, and who was sentenced to one month's hard labour in Bodmin gaol for her crimes. Another example would be George, Josiah and Philip Andrewartha, again of Breage, all convicted of assaulting John Davey, a police constable in the execution of his duty in 1831, and all sentenced to six months hard labour in Bodmin gaol. A third case involving John Andrewartha, miner of Gwennap in 1831, saw him receive nine months hard labour for stealing 100lbs of copper ore, property of Stephen Davey.

ANGOVE

Again we have the *an* prefix, this time followed by *gove,* or more correctly *gof,* meaning 'smith', as in blacksmith. Of just over 300 folk of this name in England in 1861, all but a very small number are in Cornwall and of that small number, one family in Devonshire are of Cornish extract, moving just across the Tamar to work as coppersmiths in Buckfastleigh. Perhaps the most famous or notorious Angof, depending on your point of view, was Michael Joseph, born in St Keverne and a blacksmith by trade. It was he along with Thomas Flamank of Bodmin who led the much famed Cornish Rebellion of 1497, when an estimated 15,000 strong uprising of Cornishmen marched on London in protest against taxes imposed by King Henry VII.

The whole episode was doomed to failure and on Saturday 17 June 1497, the uprising was quelled with little bloodshed. The fate of the ringleaders was finally sealed ten days later. An Gof, the Cornish

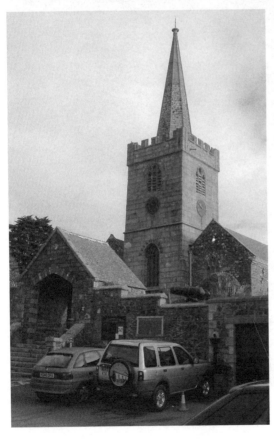

Above: The plaque, in both Cornish and English, was placed on the wall of St Keverne Churchyard in 1966 to honour the sacrifice made by Michael Joseph An Gof and Thomas Flamank in their gallant march on London in 1497.

Left: St Keverne Church.

The monument to Michael Joseph and Thomas Flamank, commissioned in 1997 to mark the 500th anniversary of the Cornish Rebellion.

blacksmith along with Thomas Flamank, a lawyer from Bodmin, and James Touchet, seventh Baron Audley from Wells, were all put to death. Lord Audley was beheaded at the Tower of London but being commoners, An Gof and Flamank suffered the fate of being hanged, drawn and quartered at Tyburn. An Gof is said to have called out as he was being dragged on a hurdle to his death that his name would be forever remembered and immortalised. This part of the story is very true as in 1997, 500 years after the original event, his march was re-enacted and a monument to his endeavours was unveiled in St Keverne. His memory lives on.

Among other prominent Angoves is Dr William Thomas Angove, general practitioner and surgeon, who qualified in medicine from the London Hospital in 1875. He married Miss Emma Carlyon in Wisbech, Cambridgeshire in 1879. Emma was the daughter of Frederick and Lucy Carlyon, both of whom were born in Truro. Her father was a well travelled churchman, and Emma was born in South Africa before the family later returned to England and Frederick became the vicar at Leverington in Cambridgeshire. More details of the Carlyon family can be found under the entry for that surname later in this book.

Emma and Thomas Angove emigrated from Mildenhall, Suffolk, where Thomas practiced medicine to Australia in 1886. He not only continued his medical career, attending the poor and the destitute in his role as district medical officer, but also began experimenting with winemaking, growing his own vines at Tea Tree Gulley in the foothills near Adelaide. His enterprise expanded from both red and white wines into the making of fortified wines, similar to port and sherry. A large Cornish-built steam boiler was installed at the plant to help in the process of making these fortified wines. Dr Angove returned to England in 1912 to carry on his medical work at the London Hospital, but he sadly died soon afterwards at the age of fifty-eight. His son, Thomas Carlyon Angove, took over and expanded the wine business in Australia, pioneering vine growing and winemaking in the Renmark irrigation settlement. One of their new products was St Agnes Brandy, named after the area in Cornwall which had been the Angove family home just before they left for Australia.

Today this business is world renowned for its fine wines.

ANGWIN

The name derives from *an gwyn,* the *gwyn* meaning 'fair' or 'white'.
Again the vast majority, over 90 per cent, of the Angwin population of
England and Wales are in Cornwall in 1861. Among those who are not,
one Cornish-born Angwin is serving in the Army and there are two
Angwin families, one in Plymouth and one in London, who are both
of Cornish origin, so here again we have a quite uniquely Cornish
surname, derived from the ancient Cornish Celtic tongue.

Of those here in Cornwall, over 85 per cent are in the far west of the
county with a definite stronghold in the parish of St Just in Penwith,
with miner as the majority occupation. A look at the parish registers
of this part of Cornwall shows that the name has been in the St Just
area since at least the earliest surviving registers of around 1600.

This is an area where many of our most famous mines are
situated. Names like Geevor, Levant, Botallack and Cape Cornwall
are synonymous with Cornish mining and, in the case of Levant in
particular, with one of the worst disasters in Cornish mining history.
On the afternoon of 20 October 1919, the man engine, a device used
to speed up the transmission of men from ground level (grass) to
working level, failed and thirty-one miners tragically died. It was at
nearby Wheal Owles on 10 January 1893 that another of Cornwall's
worst mining tragedies took place. This is a disaster we shall touch on
again later in this book under the family name of Eddy. The geology
of this area dictates that many of the West Penwith mines tunnel out
under the sea, making the work even more dangerous.

Of Angwins who have spread further than St Just, perhaps the best
known is Edwin Angwin. There is a small town bearing the name of
Angwin in the Napa Valley, California, about seventy miles or so north
of San Francisco. The town is named after Edwin Angwin, himself a St
Just man who emigrated there in the nineteenth century. One account
tells of him 'growing potatoes and preaching the Gospel'. Another
report suggests a potential business opportunity when it says, 'Mr
Angwin should make of it a resort for health and pleasure of others
and profit for himself and add to the many attractions that surround
the pleasant town of St Helena'.

It seems that Edwin Angwin took this advice and his resort became very well known. In 1909, he sold his property to the Seventh Day Adventist Church, who had outgrown their previous home in Healdsburg, California. They renamed it Pacific Union College and it continued to grow. It still functions today as a Seventh Day Adventist Liberal Arts College.

ANNEAR

Derived from *an hyr,* meaning 'tall' or 'long', this name has also evolved into Manhire and Mennear. Dealing specifically with the Annear spelling, it crops up mainly in mid-Cornwall on the 1861 census, Falmouth, Truro and Redruth being the main areas. Narrowing this down, those in the Falmouth area are to be found mainly around Budock, where the majority are stone masons. In the Truro area there is a concentration around Probus and the area towards the Roseland Peninsula around Veryan. A couple of the Probus Annear families are shoemakers by trade, whilst others are engaged in agriculture. Some of the earliest Annear names in parish registers appear in Probus, St Erme and Ladock parishes. The Redruth concentration is around the town of Redruth itself and nearby Gwennap and, as can be guessed by the locations, the main occupation is mining.

The 1935 *Who's Who of Cornwall* gives us the name of Captain Joseph Charles Annear, born in Penryn in 1896, educated at Truro College and married in 1921 to Gwendoline, daughter of William Job. He was a long term Alderman of Penryn and elected Mayor from 1929 to 1932. He was also President of the Penryn Chamber of Commerce. He served throughout the First World War in the Royal Engineers in a variety of fields of combat. His interests in the 1935 *Who's Who* are noted as the much more peaceful occupations of trout and sea fishing and golf...and perhaps not so peaceful, shooting. Penryn also had an Annear coal merchant for many years, based on the quay where ships unloaded into the coal yard and from where lorries delivered household coal to the neighbourhood.

ARGALL

The word *argel* is again from the ancient Cornish language but we have an immediate problem of a potential double meaning. T.F.G. Dexter, in his 1920s book *Cornish Names*, suggests it is from *ar* meaning 'above' and *war* meaning 'ridge', whilst a second and even third authority on the subject, Richard R. Bennett and G. Pawley White both suggest its meaning is a 'secluded place' or 'retreat'.

Having discussed the issue with one who should know, Mr Ian Argall, who has completed a comprehensive study of the name, he assures me that the generally accepted origin of the name is the second option, 'secluded place' or 'retreat'. In common with many family names, its origins are in a place name, in this case Argel, Argol, Argoll or Argal, depending on which version you prefer and what age map or document you are looking at. Its location is within the parish of Budock and it gives its name now to a reservoir, although there is still a farm with the same name nearby.

Mr Ian Argall suggests that the earliest occurrence of the place name is in 1234, which would indicate that the associated family of that name had been in the area at least as long. By the 1861 census there were about 100 in Cornwall bearing the name, whilst the family of Joseph and Mary Argall and their six children had crossed the border to Stoke Damerel in Plymouth on military duty, having been born in St Agnes.

Most of the 1861 Argalls have deserted the Falmouth area and can now be found in and around Redruth, although many seem to have migrated here from their birthplace of St Agnes on the north coast. As with most Cornish names of this era, evidence of their migration is abundant and the name is now found in USA, Australia, New Zealand and South Africa, the usual haunts of the Cornish miner. Mr Ian Argall is confident that over 97 per cent of persons bearing the Argall name have now been contacted worldwide.

The Argall name is, as has been noted, a very ancient one. Among its illustrious bearers in Cornwall was Thomas Argall, who is listed as owning the living of Crowan Rectory as far back as 1542. His heirs spread the family name to Kent in the south-east of England where in 1563, Lawrence Argal became Registrar of the Prerogative Court of Canterbury, an extremely important position dealing with the wills and estates of the great and the good of the time. It was a post formerly held by his father, Richard Argal, son of Thomas, who was married twice, and his second wife Mary, daughter of Sir Reginald Scott of Scott's Hall, Kent, who was a direct descendant of King David of Scotland. Richard's own son, Samuel, later became Sir Samuel. He purchased a knighthood in 1606 when King James was offering such honours as a means of raising money to run the country. Sir Samuel was involved in the abduction of the Powhaton princess Pocahontas in the Virginia colony in 1613, and he became Lieutenant Governor of that colony in 1617. His brother, John, joined him in the Virginia colony, and his legal training saw him as one of the signatories to the Charter of New England in 1620.

Yet another brother, Rowland Argal, also became a lawyer and among other positions was Sheriff of County Down, Ireland and Secretary to the Lord Lieutenant of Ireland.

As an aside, Princess Pocahontas is said by some to have been the inspiration for the Cornish village Indian Queens getting that name. She is said to have spent one night at the Inn there on her journey to London in 1616 with her husband, John Rolfe, after they had landed in Falmouth on their journey from America. The one problem with this story is that the official version of their journey to England has them landing in Plymouth, and as such a night at Indian Queens would have seen them travelling in the wrong direction. But who am I to scupper local legend?

Others will tell you that the name Indian Queens goes back only as far as the nineteenth century, but there is a road called Pocahontas Crescent in Indian Queens, so somebody obviously thought there was a connection or sought to keep up the legend.

The old pub sign of the Indian Queen pub, which hung in the village for many years hedged its bets on this issue and pleased both camps with a portrait of Pocahontas on one side and of Queen Victoria on the other. Good business sense I would say, keeping in with both sets of local beliefs.

BARNICOAT

Opinion is divided as to whether this name is or is not of Cornish origin. Is it from *bar an cos,* meaning 'top of the wood' or is it of non-specific and non-Cornish origin? I do not know the answer, but can offer the indication that almost 90 per cent of all those across England and Wales bearing the name in the 1861 census are living in Cornwall, whilst a second interpretation of the name in Barnecutt gives a majority living in Plymouth and West Devon, but of these some have a Cornish place of birth. Evidence of true Cornish connections? I will leave that for further debate.

Suffice to say that the Barnicoat name in Cornwall is prominent in the Truro and Falmouth areas in the mid-nineteenth century, with eight out of the thirteen adult male Barnicoats in the Falmouth area showing the occupation of mason. This occupation seems to have been handed down from father to son through several generations, beginning with Francis Barnicoat, born in 1754, who passed on the skills to his son, also Francis, born in 1795 and he to his son, John, born in 1817 and yet again to his son, Henry, who is shown as a mason at the age of fourteen years in 1861. One family member who turned his hand to an entirely different way of life was Andrew Barnicoat, son of John and younger brother to Henry, who moved away from Falmouth to Rochdale in Lancashire where he married Sarah Ann Howarth in 1878. She was from a Rochdale family with generations of experience in rope making and the cotton mills.

Charles Barnicoat, born in 1842, subsidised his mason's income in later years by becoming Inspector of Nuisances and Port Sanitary Inspector. He too passed on the masonry skills to his son, yet another Francis Barnicoat. Evidence of the Barnicoat name being associated with the building trade in the Falmouth area is available from at least the mid-nineteenth century right up to modern times.

The Truro branch of the family on the other hand is mainly involved in agriculture, with a couple of blacksmiths and a rat catcher for good measure on the 1861 census. The village of Tregony and that immediate area is the family stronghold in the Truro area. The 1935 *Who's Who of Cornwall* gives us one Barnicoat born out of Cornwall, but who lived and worked here for many years. Reverend Guy Humphry Barnicoat M.A., C.F. was born in 1888 in Lewisham, London, the son of Charles Humphry Barnicoat, a general merchant's clerk originally from Bere Alston in south Devon. Guy Barnicoat was educated at St Dunstan's College, Selwyn College, Cambridge and Wells Technical College. In 1922 he married Dora Emmeline, daughter of Thomas William Taylor, and before moving to Cornwall he was appointed assistant priest at Turnham Green in 1912, Acton Green in 1916 and Hendon in 1920. He moved to Tywardreath in Cornwall in 1925 where he founded and was first chairman of the local British Legion. He had seen action as a Military Chaplain in France and Belgium during the First World War and afterwards in Germany.

BASSETT

The name of Bassett is firmly associated with the Tehidy Estate which is situated in the heart of the old Cornish mining area around Camborne and Redruth. The estate itself covered a rather modest 250 acres but the Bassett name is seen on countless land deeds, tenancy agreements and other property documents right across Cornwall and far beyond.

The family name first appears as far back as the Battle of Hastings where there is mention of both the Bassett name, in the shape of Thurston Basset, and the de Dunstanville name fighting alongside William and upon his victory, being granted lands and estates across the country. Both of these names are linked to the Bassett of Tehidy dynasty. As far back as the year 1100, Alan de Dunstanville was Lord of the Manor in the area where Tehidy now stands. His daughter, Cecelia, married William Basset of Ipsden in Oxfordshire, and so ever since the two names have been linked to Cornwall and to Tehidy. Down the centuries many Bassett names have been associated with wealth and high office. The family were granted the right to hold a market in Redruth as far back as 1330. Sir Francis Bassett, born in 1594, bought St Michael's Mount in 1640 and became High Sheriff of Cornwall in 1644, an honour conferred by the King himself at Boconnoc. The family were firm Royalists during these dark days in English history and as a result lost St Michael's Mount again, firstly to Commonwealth forces in 1646 and in the following year, they were forced to sell the Mount to the St Aubyn family to help pay considerable personal debts incurred in support of the Royalist cause during the Civil War. Family members have represented the area in Parliament, although not always voted for in the way we would select an MP today.

The 1861 census has a total of almost 3,000 Bassetts spread far and wide across England and Wales and only about 10 per cent of these live in Cornwall. Neither are they all of the aristocratic classes. Listed among their occupations are agricultural labourer, carter, railway labourer, tin dresser and even pauper. Our own Tehidy Bassett family of the time, Gustavus Bassett with his wife, Charlotte, appear to have spent far more time in their London home at Hanover Square and at other grand addresses around the country than they ever did living at Tehidy. Perhaps this was because Gustavus was not the most well-liked landlord. His word was law. Greed and an autocratic approach were his in abundance whilst common sense and listening to those who seemed to know what they were talking about were not among his assets. Poor decisions included the sinking of a new shaft at Dolcoath mine, for example, which those in the know said was a waste of money, and the banning of miners' picnics on sites they had used for this purpose for generations. These were not the actions of a man who sought to endear himself to his fellow beings. His son Arthur, who later took over the estate, was perhaps even worse. It took him just over twenty years to go from a life of wealth and luxury at Tehidy to selling the family jewellery and finally the estate itself to pay massive debts, mostly incurred through his gambling addiction. 'It's the horses you know,' is said to have been his final word on the demise of the centuries-old dynasty as he left in 1915. Perhaps these later generations of the Bassett family would have done better had they remembered their centuries-old family motto of *Pro Rege et Populo,* which translates as 'for King and People'. Since the early twentieth century the house at Tehidy has seen a variety of uses, from tuberculosis hospital to luxury apartments. The grounds today are laid out as a country park with many pleasant walks where the aristocracy once roamed.

Not all of the Bassetts of Tehidy were bad characters. Francis Bassett, for example, was a great patron of John Opie, the Cornish artist in the late eighteenth century and was a pall bearer at Opie's funeral in 1807, and it is this same Francis who is remembered on the monument on the summit of Carn Brea Hill. Visible for miles around, this 90ft tall granite monument was built by public subscription in 1836 in fond

Above: The inscription on the Basset monument reads, 'The County of Cornwall to the Memory of Francis Lord de Dunstanville and Basset AD 1836'.

Left: The Basset Monument on the top of Carn Brea Hill near Redruth stands some 90ft high and was erected in honour of Francis Basset, Lord de Dunstanville, after his death in 1835.

Carn Brea Castle. Originally built as a fourteenth-century chapel, it was extended and modified by the Basset family in the eighteenth century. One corner of the castle stands on top of the natural rock formation of the hill.

memory of a man who did so much for Cornish mining…and of course enhanced his own fortunes at the same time.

But all that aside, is the name Cornish? It has been suggested that the name derives from the Celtic word *bassya* meaning 'short' or 'shallow', but it does not, in my opinion, seem to have any firm recognisable links to the Celtic tongue, as do many of the other names we are looking at. Having been in the county since 1066 and all that, I suppose it qualifies in that way and so it is included here.

BASTIAN

From one name which we have said may not be Cornish but is found in abundance right across the county, we move to another which is almost uniquely Cornish. There are 118 Bastian names on the 1861 census of England and Wales and with the exception of one family in Middlesex, one in Hertfordshire and another just across the border in Plymouth, all are in Cornwall. The name does not seem to have any particular origins in the Celtic tongue and it has been suggested that it is simply a shortened form of Sebastian. But why here in Cornwall in such a large percentage? Perhaps because of our close links with France and the Iberian Peninsula, where the name Sebastian is found as a personal name and in place names. Historically the name comes from St Sebastian, a Christian martyr of the third century who, despite being arrested, tied to a tree and shot at with dozens of arrows as punishment for his Christian faith, survived to denounce Emperor Diocletian for his persecution of Christians. For this he was arrested again and this time put to death by being beaten with cudgels.

Hopefully no such fate ever befell any Cornish Bastians. They seem to have been a mainly hard-working bunch. The Coverack, Porthallow and St Keverne area is home to Bastians engaged in farming. Crowan has Bastians engaged in mining and other occupations include mariner, sail maker and blacksmith.

One Bastian not in Cornwall in 1861 is Henry Charlton Bastian. Born in 1837 in Cornwall, the son of Henry Bastian, a copper miner from Kerley Downs in Kea parish, and his wife Ann, formerly Ann Northey, Henry is said to have had a very keen interest in natural history from an early age and to have shown much promise and a keen mind. He proved these talents by becoming a graduate of the University of London in 1861 and can be found in the census of that year working as a medical lecturer in London. Exactly how the son of a Cornish miner rose to such heights is something of a mystery but undoubtedly his talents were recognised by a wealthy sponsor, for a miner's wages would not meet the cost of such an education as he received.

He married Julia Orme, daughter of Charles Orme, also a medical man, and his wife Eliza in 1866, and they had three sons, Charles, James and William and two daughters, May and Sybil.

By complete contrast, Henry's parents left Cornwall like so many thousands of others when mining was in severe decline and emigrated to Kapunda, about fifty miles north of Adelaide and renowned for being the oldest copper mining town in Australia.

Meanwhile back in London, Henry junior was making quite a name for himself as a physiologist and neurologist. He was made a Fellow of the Royal Society in 1868.

He became a physician at University College Hospital, London, in 1878 and also worked at the National Hospital in Queens Square, London, from 1868 to 1902. He was awarded an honorary fellowship of the Royal College of Physicians of Ireland and an honorary MD from the Royal University of Ireland. He acted for the Crown in cases of alleged insanity for many years and, just before his death in 1915, he was awarded a pension of £150 a year from the Civil List in recognition of his services to medicine. Perhaps his greatest legacy is his work with speech disorders. As early as 1869 he gave the first ever account of word blindness and of word deafness, known today as Wernicke's Aphasia. He also discovered the anterior spinocerebellar tract of the spinal chord, now known as Gowers' tract because of later work on the same subject by Sir William Richard Gowers.

His work in this area led in 1890 to Bastian's Law, which proved that severing of the upper spinal chord eliminates reflexes and muscular activity causing paralysis below the level of the spinal lesion.

He was the last scientific champion and campaigner for the causes of abiogenesis and archebiosis, the belief that living things arise from inorganic or inanimate matter or from dead animals and plant matter. He argued that there was no strict boundary between organic and inorganic life, believing that living matter must have originated from non-living matter at a very early stage of evolution and as such, the same process may still be ongoing.

Henry Charlton Bastian died on 17 November 1915 and received the honour of an obituary in *The Lancet* and the *British Medical Journal.* This was a far cry from his humble beginnings amongst the smoking mine chimneys on Kerley Downs.

BEHENNA

Here we have another name probably derived in two parts from the old Celtic tongue. *Be* or *Bos* is 'dwelling' and *henna* or *hendra* is 'old', so the folk who live in the 'old dwelling' or 'old farm'. There are alternative suggestions given that it is simply from *Bod Hannah,* 'dwelling of Hannah' or that an element of it may derive from *byghan,* meaning 'small'. The one Behenna I can remember from my own childhood days was, however, far from small. He was a large man, our local blacksmith, and affectionately known as Cap'n Behenna, as he had seen considerable military service. Sadly he died of injuries sustained in a road accident after being hit by a car whilst riding his bicycle.

Whichever is the true meaning of the name, it is found almost exclusively in Cornwall. The name occurs in various parts of the county but the main stronghold appears to be in the Truro area, going out onto the Roseland Peninsula towards Merther, St Just in Roseland and Gerrans. A variety of trades and occupations are followed, including blacksmith, carpenter, tailor, rope maker and grocer. There is also Ferdinando Behenna who ran a pawnbroker's shop in River Street, Truro, next to the former Baptist Church for more than thirty years. He was the son of another Ferdinando who in his time was an innkeeper at Kea and was also overseer of the poor of Kea parish.

BIDDICK

This is a name found as far back as the *Bodmin Manumissions* or *Bodmin Gospels* we mentioned in the introduction, which possibly predates the Norman invasion by as much as 150 years. These writings give details of the freeing of slaves from their masters and the entries read along the lines of, 'Here are the names of the slaves who XXX frees for the sake of his soul.' These records provide some of the earliest written references to names which survive in Cornwall. *Budic* appears here as the name of a freed male slave and it is generally accepted that this is the origin of the name Biddick. Its Celtic meaning is 'victorious' and the female version of the name is *Budica,* which has its origins at least as far back as the legendary Queen Budica or Boadicea of the first century AD. Reference to the name can also be found in ancient Breton documents of this era.

It is a name which, although it appears in a variety of places across Cornwall in the nineteenth century, is particularly associated with the parishes of St Merryn, St Issey and St Ervan where most Biddick families are engaged in farming. There are still Biddick family engaged in farming in this same area today and evidence through leases and land records show that the name has been associated with farming here for at least three centuries.

Two sons of John Warne Biddick, gentleman farmer of St Merryn, served with distinction in the 1914-1918 First World War and served their local community in a variety of ways in peacetime. The first, Captain John Biddick, was born in 1863, educated at Brown's Private School, Padstow, and qualified as a Master Mariner. He served as Commander of Admiralty Transport from 1914-1916 and after the war, held a variety of local positions, including membership of St Columb Parish Council and the National Lifeboat Committee. His younger brother, Edwy, was a Captain in the Mercantile Marine throughout the First World War, survived two torpedo attacks from German submarines in the Mediterranean Sea whilst on convoy duty, received the Admiralty's Parchment Certificate of Thanks for Meritorious Service after the war and was also presented with the War Service and Mercantile Marine Medals.

BLIGHT

This is a name which is more West Country than just Cornish, as there are almost as many Blight names, with slight variations in spelling, to be found in neighbouring Devonshire as there are in Cornwall. The name, and its main variations of Blyth and Bligh, are rooted in the Celtic word *Blyth,* meaning 'wolf'. It is a name spread across the county from Stratton in the north east to St Germans in the south east, and all the way down to Penzance in the far west.

One rather sad tale from Blight family history surrounds the life of John Thomas Blight. He was born in 1835, the eldest son of schoolmaster Robert Blight, who was originally from St Germans, and his wife, Thomasine. The Blight family settled in Madron, near Penzance, where Robert was a schoolmaster for over thirty years. John and his younger brother Joseph, with help from their father, began a study of their new surroundings, sketching the ancient crosses and other antiquities of the area and learning a great deal about its history and unique character. John became an accomplished artist and his first book, a lavishly illustrated work entitled *Ancient Crosses and Antiquities of Cornwall* was offered on subscription only in 1856 to a select number of the great and the good of Cornish society. This drew Blight the attention and patronage of Richard Hawker, the vicar of Morwenstow, who encouraged his work on the study of Cornwall's ancient crosses and other relics. As a result, a second volume on crosses and antiquities in east Cornwall was published two years later. Sadly though, Blight and Hawker disagreed and their ways parted. A second patron, academic James Orchard Halliwell-Phillips, then encouraged Blight and he was commissioned as the illustrator for an edition of Halliwell-Phillips' *Life of Shakespeare* for which Blight spent months in Stratford drawing the places and buildings there relevant to Shakespeare's life and times. Payment for this was poor and he was forced into accepting other commissions and working far too long hours just to pay his way. His inability to cope with the stresses and strains which this put upon him began to have an adverse effect on his state of mind. He is at home with his parents in Penzance on the 1871 census, with an occupation of 'author of antiquities', but very soon after this he became an in-patient at the County Asylum in Bodmin where he spent the rest of his life. Although his stay there was eased by being treated as a private inmate, thanks to sums of money raised by his many friends and admirers of his work, it was still a sad waste of a life which had promised so much and which, with the correct backing, could have achieved great heights. It was reported at one time that John Blight had died in 1884 but recent evidence suggests that he lived on until 1911.

Another, somewhat mysterious and certainly different bearer of the Blight name was Tamson Blight. Born around 1798 in Helston, she married James Thomas, a mine engine driver. Both are said to have had the power of healing, although 'professional differences' seem to have led to a rather stormy relationship. Tamson, or Tammy Blee as she was better known, had the power of healing and could banish curses put upon folk by witches and other dark dwellers, and cure ills in both humans and animals by the laying on of her hands. When she lay dying, many were brought to her deathbed by their relatives on stretchers and after a few minutes in her presence were apparently cured and well enough to walk unaided down the stairs and out into the street, singing her praises.

The Bligh or Blight name is also long associated with the town of Bodmin, for many centuries Cornwall's principle town. A succession of Blight names are to be found amongst the list of Mayors of the town from as far back as Richard Bligh, born in 1452, who was Mayor of Bodmin in 1505 and again in 1521. John, his son, took the office in 1531 and 1539. He had married Johanna Colquite, a name still associated with that area, whose family connections included the Rashleigh family of Fowey. John's son, also John, was Mayor of Bodmin in 1582 and 1588 and others have included Thomas Blight, 1559 and 1570, Charles Blight, 1659 and 1678, Francis Blight, Notary Public and Mayor in 1674 and 1684, and Lewis Blight, 1734 and 1741.

Perhaps the best known of all the bearers of the name though is Admiral William Bligh. His early years are the subject of some debate among historians and researchers. One version says he was born in 1753 in Plymouth, the son of John Bligh of St Kew, another that he was born in 1754 at Tinten, St Tudy, the son of Charles and Margaret Bligh, and yet a third confirms the St Tudy connection but has his parents as Francis and Jane. Even Walter Tregellas, in his 1884 work *Some Cornish Worthies*, admits that there is 'some uncertainty' in his parentage. Tinten, as an aside, is a very ancient manor in St Tudy dating from the time of Edward I in the thirteenth century and has been in the ownership of both the Carminow and Courtenay families of that area for several centuries. Whatever the truth of William Bligh's earliest years, he joined the Royal Navy at a very early age, perhaps as young as seven years old, a common practice to hasten promotion of young officers. He rose quickly through the ranks, his first appointment as Master coming in 1776 aboard the sloop HMS *Resolution*. He married Betsy Betham, daughter of a customs officer in 1781 and later that year saw active service at the Battle of Dogger Bank under Admiral Parker. The following year he was on active service under Lord Howe at Gibraltar and for a few years after that was Captain of several vessels in the Merchant Service. He returned to the Royal Navy in 1787 where he took command of HMS *Bounty* and the rest, as they say, is history, extremely well-documented history, not only written about but made into films by Hollywood and the subject on many artists' canvases. After this episode, Bligh saw many further years of service with the Royal Navy before taking a shore post as Governor of New South Wales. He returned from that to England, was promoted to Rear Admiral and ultimately to Vice Admiral.

This Cornish boy had a career as adventurous as anyone could wish for, perhaps too much so on occasions. He died on 6 December 1817 and was buried in St Mary's Church, Lambeth.

BOASE

Another name that is formed in two parts from the old Celtic language. *Bo* is also found as Bos, Bus, Bod or Bot and means 'dwelling' or 'home'. The second part here is derived from the Celtic word *res* meaning 'ford'. So here we have dwellers by the ford in the river. River crossings were very important meeting places in the days before knowledge and building materials allowed bridges across wide rivers. Many settlements here in Cornwall and around the world have developed at the lowest fording point of rivers. Truro, for example is the lowest easy crossing point on the Fal estuary. Boase is a name found in various parts of Cornwall but it is mainly associated with the Penzance area in the west of the county. Occupations vary, with examples of the Boase family working as miners in and around Lelant and St Ives, farmers in St Buryan and fishermen in Newlyn. All traditional occupations which their fathers, and probably several generations before them, would have followed.

Of the few Boase families on the 1861 census and not in Cornwall, some have their roots here. One of interest is Edward Boase, a newspaper reporter born in Falmouth who is living in Liverpool with his family on this census. He was the son of Edward and Margaret Boase. He married Jane Louisa Ivory Andrew in Falmouth in 1839 and they moved to Penzance, where he is listed on the 1844 *Pigot's Trade Directory* as the proprietor of the *Penzance Gazette and West Cornwall Advertiser*. His wife was a school teacher and the family remained in Penzance until the early 1850s when they moved to Bristol, where their only son, Herbert, was born. They later moved to Liverpool. Two of their daughters, Julia and Ellen, became accomplished music teachers, whilst their third daughter, Jessie, followed in the family footsteps and became a printer and compositor. Sadly though, Edward's life was to end in poverty, as an inmate of the West Derby Workhouse in Liverpool.

Other than Edward, there have been Boase family members who have made their name in a wide variety of professions. John Josias Arthur Boase was a banker and landowner. The name of Henry Boase of Penzance is also associated with banking. He became a partner in the former Oxnam, Batten & Co. bank in 1810 and the bank was renamed Batten, Carne & Boase. It remained as such until Henry's retirement in 1823 when it became Batten, Carne & Carne. John Boase's son, Charles William, was a man of the church. George Boase, of the same family line, became an author and bibliographer and Frederick Boase, also originally from Penzance, became a successful solicitor, and the name of Boase can still be found in the legal profession in Penzance to this day. William Henry Boase is also listed in the 1844 *Pigot's Trade Directory* of Penzance as a ship owner whilst Francis Boase of Penzance was a noted surgeon. His Boase family were related to the Millett family and several medical men of note have come from this branch of the name, perhaps most notably George Millett M.R.C.S. In addition to his medical duties, he found time to write two volumes on the history of Penzance, transcribe Madron and Gulval parish registers and lend his support to a variety of charitable and voluntary organisations of Victorian Cornwall.

BOLITHO

Again the first part is *Bo* meaning house or dwelling but the second part, depending on which reference work you look at, is suggested as possibly from any one of three different Celtic words, *Lethyow,* meaning 'dairy', *Leath,* meaning 'damp place' or *Leghow,* meaning 'slabs of rock'. Why such a wide variance, you might ask? The answer is simply that as with all names of this age, they have evolved over centuries. In those earlier centuries there were few scholars and nobody wrote down a definitive glossary or lexicon of words and their meaning which has survived to the modern era. Not that it would have had too many customers; for the vast majority of folk in Cornwall, and indeed elsewhere in England, learning to read and write several centuries ago was not something they ever thought of. It was not until the Victorian era that we find schooling and learning to read and write beginning to creep in as a necessary or even obligatory activity.

The name Bolitho can claim to be one of those names which is truly Cornish, despite the apparent differences of opinion amongst modern day scholars as to its origins.

On the 1861 census, nearly 95 per cent of the Bolitho names are here in Cornwall and a few who are not have birth places here and are working elsewhere. About 50 per cent of the Cornish Bolitho names are in the Helston area, with others spread from Towednack in the west to Callington in the east.

Bolitho's bank is a firm part of Cornish history. Established in 1807 by the brothers Thomas and William Bolitho as Mount's Bay Commercial Bank and based at Chyandour, its name changed in 1810 to Bolitho, Sons & Co. In 1834 the bank moved to premises in Market Jew Street in the centre of Penzance and was renamed the Mount's Bay Bank.

In 1838, Richard Foster Bolitho, only son of one of the founding partners, William Bolitho, together with his two cousins, Thomas Simon Bolitho and Edward Bolitho, sons of Thomas, the other founder, took over the running of the bank. Another William Bolitho, who in later life continued in his banking career despite the onset of blindness, and a second Thomas Bolitho are to be found in the next generation of bankers and by now branches had been opened in St Ives, St Just, Hayle and St Mary's on the Scilly Isles. Richard Foster Bolitho, grandson of the original William, was also involved in the banking business as well as being a local magistrate and Deputy Lieutenant of Cornwall. The family became known as the 'Merchant Princes' of Cornwall, for not only did they have interests in banking but also in other areas, not least in the tin smelting business. The Bolitho family branch at Penryn became tanners and general merchants, increasing and widening the family business portfolio.

The census of 1881 shows no less than five Bolitho family members involved in the banking business in Penzance, with addresses which were, and still are, substantial properties on the outskirts of the town. One property in Bolitho ownership from 1867 was Trengwainton House, set high above the town with unrivalled and uninterrupted

Lanyon Quoit on the Penwith Moors, an ancient relic of the pre-Christian era. It stands on land once owned by the Bolitho family and a plaque nearby tells that Lanyon Quoit was given to the National Trust by Sir Edward Bolitho of Trengwainton in 1952.

views out over Mount's Bay. The origins of a house on this site date back several centuries but the Bolitho family bought it from Sir Rose Price, a former Jamaican sugar planter, who was the first to set out much of the formal gardens. He built a series of raised and walled beds, designed in such a way that they gained maximum protection from the often severe Cornish weather coming in off the Atlantic Ocean and were angled towards the winter sun to provide maximum warmth and daylight. The Bolitho family were not renowned for their interest in having a great botanical garden until the house was inherited in 1925 by Edward Bolitho. He took a keen interest in the gardens and sponsored Frank Kingdon-Ward, noted botanist, explorer, plant collector and author in his late 1920s expeditions to exotic locations, including Burma and Assam, from where he brought back a host of plant specimens new to Britain, many of which found their way to Trengwainton's gardens.

Sadly though, tragedy does not distinguish between the gentry and the common man in times of war and there are three Bolitho family names on the War Memorial at Madron. Lieutenant William Torquill McLeod Bolitho, son of Lieutenant Colonel William Edward Thomas

Bolitho, DSO was killed in action on 24 May 1915 at the age of just twenty-two. His name is also with so many thousands of others on the Menin Gate at Ypres, which commemorates the fallen who have no known grave. His father is also on that same Madron memorial, he died in February 1919 of a war-related illness. The third Bolitho name there is that of Second Lieutenant Geoffrey Richard Bolitho, son of Edward Bolitho of Trengwainton, a Royal Navy Commander and coastguard of Penzance.

No book on Cornish folk would be complete, I dare to offer, without a musical note or two. One such can be fitted in here in the name of John Bolitho. He was born in Bude in 1930, the son of the local butcher and his working life began with ten years in the Royal Navy. He later settled in London and engaged in that familiar passion of so many Cornishmen, singing. This led to an audition with George Mitchell and eventually to a twelve-year spell with *The Black and White Minstrel Show,* which included two Royal Command Performance engagements. In 1970 he returned to his native north Cornwall to live and work and to take an ever more passionate role in all things Cornish. He became a Bard of the Cornish Gorseth and was a councillor in Bude for many years. He stood as a Mebyon Kernow candidate for North Cornwall in a Parliamentary election and became the first man to deliver a speech in the Cornish language before the European Parliament. In 2002 he was installed as Grand Bard of the Gorseth and during his time in office he was the voice of Cornwall, in more ways than one, on a worldwide basis wherever Cornish folk gathered to celebrate their identity. He died in December 2005 at the age of seventy-four.

BORLASE

Another two-part name, derived from *Bor*, meaning 'embankment' and *glas*, meaning 'green'. A similar alternative meaning of 'the high green summit' is also suggested. Walter Tregellas, in his 1884 work *Some Cornish Worthies,* suggests that the name has its origins with the Norman Conquest in the name of Taillefor and that it may be 'connected to him who is reported to have struck the first blow at the Battle of Hastings'. He goes on to say that 'The Manor of Borlase-Burgess, formerly the seat of the Borlase family in St Wenn [north Cornwall] is said to have

been given by William Rufus to a certain Norman who was Lord
of Talfer and whose posterity assumed the name of Borlase'. So yet
again we see the Norman invasion being suggested as an origin as well
as a perfectly sound Celtic alternative. Perhaps the name Borlase was
chosen by the Norman landowner as a descriptive name for his lands
from the Celtic native tongue of those around him. That seems to
cover all the angles quite nicely. Who was the first Borlase, or the first
of a name similar in sound or origin, we may never know, but for our
purposes here we can say that the name crops up across Cornwall and
with a wide variety of trades and occupations.

Perhaps the most well documented Borlase was William Borlase,
born in Pendeen in 1695 into a family of some wealth and status in
the community, he was educated to university standard and graduated
from Exeter College, Oxford. He became the vicar of the parishes
of Ludgvan and St Just in Penwith, but it is probably for his writings
on Cornwall that he is best remembered. These included *Antiquities
of Cornwall,* written in 1754 and *Observations of the Ancient and Present
State of the Isles of Scilly* but perhaps his most remembered work, *The
Natural History of Cornwall,* came along in 1758. Borlase had been
made a Fellow of the Royal Society in 1750. He married Ann Smith
in Ludgvan in 1724 and they had six sons, two of whom died in
childhood. Incidentally, it is said that the last native wolf ever to be
seen in England was sighted at Rospieth in the parish of Ludgvan.
But to return to the Borlase family, it was not all fame and fortune.
William's father almost lost the family fortune through poor financial
management and this failure to manage their money seems to have
dogged the Borlase family down several generations. Three of William
and Ann's sons followed their father into the church as a career, but
sad to say all three accrued large debts. A fourth son, Christopher,
joined the Royal Navy but sadly died of fever at the age of twenty-
one. A great great grandson of William Borlase, one William Copeland
Borlase, also got himself into deep financial troubles. He was privately
educated at Winchester and then attended Trinity College, Oxford.
He married Alice Lucy Kent, the twenty-one year old daughter of a
Gloucestershire vicar in 1870 and later became MP for St Austell, but
the *West Briton* of 14 November 1887 carries the headline:'Bankruptcy
of Mr W. C. Borlase, another adjournment'

It appears that Mr Borlase had previously appeared before the
bankruptcy court and obtained an adjournment on the grounds that
'the debtor was obliged to go abroad for the benefit of his health'.

Ludgvan Church, where William Borlase was vicar for many years in the eighteenth century.

The court was told that he was still in Ireland and 'required £10 to enable him to come over to this country.' Mr Wolff, the solicitor who appeared on behalf of 'a large creditor' was, not surprisingly, outraged by this and protested that 'the sooner it was shown that Members of Parliament were not allowed to treat the Court in the way Mr Borlase had, the better for all.' Being in contempt of court was a serious offence but Mr Borlase was given one last chance to appear later in the month. The full details of the bankruptcy hearing are to be found in the same newspaper on 5 December when its sub-heading reads *'Painful disclosures in the London Bankruptcy Court'* and it then reports that:

> Before Mr Registrar Gifford, Mr W. C. Borlase of Laregan, Cornwall and late M.P. for St Austell Division, was called upon to undergo his public examination as a bankrupt. Mr Brown appeared on behalf of the trustee, Mr Aldridge for the Official Receiver, Mr Wolff for Madame Louise de Quiros, a creditor and Mr Terrell for the debtor. The accounts filed showed gross liabilities of £42,653 of which £19,037 is unsecured and assets £6,571.

This amounts to a deficit in the region of £3million when converted to today's purchasing power. Following his bankruptcy, William Copeland Borlase was disowned by his family and went back to Ireland, where he had apparently been for the sake of his health at the time of the adjourned hearing. Like his more famous ancestor before him, he wrote a number of books and articles on dolmens and other antiquities of Ireland, which are very similar in nature to those he would have known well from his years in the Penwith area of Cornwall. He died at the comparatively young age of fifty-one in 1899. The case also seems to have been the end of his marriage to Lucy as she returned to live with her parents in Coln St Aldwins, a little village near Cirencester in Gloucestershire. She eventually moved to London where she died in 1924.

One of this same generation of the Borlase family did, however, uphold the family name and standing in the community. Walter Henry Borlase, born in Penzance in 1853, was Mayor of Penzance in 1888, Clerk to the West Penwith Justices for many years from 1890, Registrar of the County Court from 1906-1921 and Under Sheriff of Cornwall in 1884, 1890 and 1892. In his spare time, according to *Who's Who of Cornwall,* he enjoyed the usual gentlemanly pursuits of hunting, shooting, walking and gardening.

BOSANKO

Bos, meaning 'dwelling' and *an cow* meaning 'death', or possibly *an coys* meaning 'wooded area', are the two components of this name. One source suggests that the name goes back as far as the Black Death in 1349 when whole communities were wiped out by the disease and so 'dwelling of death' or 'dwellers in the place of death' may have come into use as a name. Perhaps to carry a name meaning 'dwelling of death' is not as attractive as one meaning 'dwelling by the wooded area' but opinion is divided and I am not qualified to make the ultimate judgement. With the exception of one family of lead miners in South Wales, the whole Bosanko population of England and Wales is in Cornwall in 1861 and even the family in Wales have a Cornish place of birth, so it is one of those names which can truly be said to be Cornish. In fact, about a third of the total Bosanko population are to be found in Sithney parish, with another goodly number in the adjoining parishes of Crowan and Wendron, and naturally for this part of Cornwall, the majority occupation is mining.

Like many Cornish names, Bosanko is now to be found in parts of the world most associated with mining. South Australia was one destination, North America was another and also South Africa. The old saying that wherever in the world you find a hole in the ground you will find a Cornishman is certainly true of the Bosanko name.

BOTTRELL

This is a name of uncertain origins but most agree that it is a name which can trace its presence in Cornwall back to the Norman invasion. Following his success, William divided the kingdom amongst those who had given support to his cause and one of these was Edward de Bottreaux. His son, William de Bottreaux, is thought to have built Bottreaux Castle, now shortened to Boscastle, around the end of the twelfth century. The Bottreaux or Botrell family were originally from southern Brittany. The castle fell into disrepair by the end of the fifteenth century and little now remains except for a few earthworks just visible adjacent to a modern car park. Perhaps the family line in that part of north east Cornwall died out or moved away because the name is found in more modern times almost exclusively in the Penzance area and further west towards Land's End. Perhaps these Bottrell families were the result of a later Breton invasion? After all, trade between west Cornwall and Brittany has been ongoing for many centuries and perhaps some stayed behind. We may never know the answer to that question, but what we can say for certain is that in the 1860s the Bottrell family, with a variety of spelling interpretations, are shown as miners, mariners, farmers and small businessmen.

Perhaps one of the more famous bearers of the name was born at Raftra in St Levan parish in March 1816. He was William Bottrell, son of William and Margaret Bottrell, yeoman farmers of St Levan parish for several generations. The Bottrell family had married into the Vingoe family and it was Granny Vingoe who had a great influence on young William's early years. She told tales of her family and others in the area which had been handed down by word of mouth for generations. These were later to form the basis of three volumes of folk tales written by William Bottrell. Being the only child of a fairly well-to-do family, William received an education at Penzance Grammar School and later at Bodmin School. Here he took a keen interest in classics and mathematics. By the late 1830s, William began his travels which took him to the Basque region of Spain where he purchased land and gathered folk stories of that area. His land was later confiscated by the Catholic Church and William found himself back in Cornwall, penniless. But he soon picked himself up, dusted himself down and made for Quebec in Canada, where in 1847 he obtained employment as an English teacher. Academic life did not suit him and he was soon wandering far and wide in the virgin forests of this vast land, obtaining employment with a timber company before returning again to Cornwall. His next adventure took him to Australia but sadly his young wife died there, and his spirit of adventure passed with her and again he was back in Cornwall. He lived, apparently with a cow, a pony and a black cat called Spriggans at Hawke's Point, Lelant, where he scraped a living from the land. He befriended many of the local miners and through them increased his collection of stories and legends of the area. Some of his stories first came to print in two books, not by his own hand but by that of Robert Hunt, whose volumes *Popular Romances of the West of England* were published in the 1860s. Soon afterwards, Bottrell himself was in print in *The Cornish Telegraph* newspaper and other publications of the time and earned some financial reward for his stories. Sadly he did not live to reap the full benefits of his success as a writer, as he died at the age of sixty-five in 1881 after suffering a stroke. It is a testament to his writing talent that William Bottrell's books, including *Hearthside Stories of West Cornwall* with stories of giants and the ghostly goings-on and legends of west Cornwall, remain in demand to this day.

BOWDEN

Again, *Bo* as in 'dwelling', this time perhaps with *din* or *dyn* added, meaning 'hill fort', but again, scholarly minds differ. We have many names here in Cornwall where those who have studied their origins have a variance of opinion on original meaning. It is one of the difficulties in modernising an ancient, almost extinct, language where sometimes so little written evidence remains. This is not in any way detracting from the studious research of many Cornish scholars down the years but does explain why sometimes there can be an alternative, equally well-researched and well-argued suggestion as to the origin. The name of Bowden, often seen as Bawden, is one such example. In fact, the Bawden version is almost twice as common as the Bowden version of the spelling.

It is a name spread far and wide across the county, encompassing an equally wide variety of occupations. It is also a very ancient name. Our first example of a famous bearer of the name is William Bawden. Born in Cornwall around 1563, he studied at Oxford and later at the University of Douai in northern France before moving on to Reims. He completed his studies for the priesthood in Rome and was ordained in 1586. He spent time in Rome after his ordination before moving to become a professor of theology at the Catholic University of Leuven in Belgium. His travels around Europe brought him to Germany where in 1605 he was arrested and implicated in the notorious Gunpowder Plot, when a group of English Catholics tried to blow up the King and his Parliament, giving rise to our present day Guy Fawkes celebrations. Bawden was imprisoned in the Tower of

London for several years where, despite being tortured, he offered no confession. As a result, his innocence was proclaimed and he returned to mainland Europe where he ended his days as Rector of the French Jesuit College of St Omer.

Another, perhaps less pious, bearer of the Bawden name was one Edward Bawden of Gwithian who, as the *Cornwall Gazette* reports on 25 April 1801 was before Lord Kenyon at the Old Bailey for 'wilfully and maliciously firing off a gun loaded with gunpowder and a leaden bullet at John Arnold on 6 September at Gwithian in the County of Cornwall'. Mr Arnold was a customs officer and he had been to Bawden's house earlier in the day looking for concealed smuggled goods, but had found nothing. Late in the evening of the same day, he returned with some of his Dragoons to make a further search when he alleged that he heard a man's voice he recognised as that of Bawden call out: 'the damned light horsemen are here again, shoot them.'

Shots were fired but no one was hurt. Other witnesses for the prosecution told that they had heard shots but could not corroborate Arnold's story about hearing the voice of Edward Bawden giving the instruction to 'shoot them'. For the defence, four witnesses came forward, all of whom said that they had been helping Bawden all day to bring in the harvest and had retired to his house in the evening for supper and drinks. They recalled hearing the shots but to a man told how Bawden himself had got up, braced himself against the door and said that no one should go outside for fear of being hurt. They all resumed their drinking and remained at Bawden's house until the early hours of the next morning, celebrating a successful harvest. They all swore, on oath, that Bawden had not left his house from before eight in the evening to at least six the following morning. The newspaper reports that 'Lord Kenyon summed up with much impartiality and laid down the law in a clear and distinct manner. The Jury, without the least hesitation, acquitted the prisoner.' Perhaps the headline should be 'Cornishman evades justice'? We will never know.

Other Bowden or Bawden names to appear with perhaps more distinction than that of Edward have included Major Frank Melville Bawden, M.B.E. who served with the 5th D.C.L.I. in Egypt and Palestine from 1915-1920 and was a close associate of Lord Allenby in Egypt from 1918-1920 and later made quite a name for himself at rifle shooting.

Percy Reynolds Bawden, a Redruth man through and through, made major contributions to such organisations as the Chamber of Commerce and Redruth Literary Institution, but perhaps best remembered is his work with the Redruth Victoria Jubilee Park which he helped to maintain and improve as a long-serving secretary and committee member.

Lieutenant Colonel William Arthur Bawden, J. P., after service in France from 1915-1918 with the D.C.L.I., took up a career in banking and later gave his talents as a Justice of the Peace for over thirty years, was Mayor of Bodmin on three occasions and chief officer of the Bodmin fire brigade for twenty-five years.

A wide variety of service in all aspects of public life by some bearers of the name which, like many Cornish names, is to be found all over the world today.

BRAY

Brea in the Celtic tongue means 'hill'. No problem with the meaning and origins of this Cornish name. Or is there? One reference suggests that the name is yet another which can be traced to William the Conqueror and his dividing up of his new kingdom amongst those who helped his invasion. One of these was Guillaume de Bray (William of Bray), the Bray here being the Pays de Bray, a region of north-eastern France in the triangle between the modern towns of Dieppe, Bouvais and Amiens. At its centre is the small town of Neufchatel-en-Bray, once the capital of this agricultural region. Perhaps its most famous asset is its cheese, which, like many good French cheeses, and indeed wines, has an official *appellation de origine controlle* so that it can only be named as Neufchatel if it is produced in the locality. The cheese is often sold in a heart shape, apparently because the maidens of the village offered it in this shape to the gallant heroes of the One Hundred Years War. Legend has it that on eating the cheese, the soldiers thought they were in heaven as the shape reminded them of angels' wings. Perhaps this is a more romantic origin than the Celtic for 'hill', but not one universally accepted.

Again it is a name found far and wide across Cornwall, with over 1,500 on the 1861 census. But ask any Cornishman who the most famous bearer of the name was and you are certain to hear the name of Billy Bray, preacher, miner and reformed drunkard. Billy Bray was born at Twelveheads in Kea parish near Truro on 1 June 1794. His father died when he was a young boy and his formative years were spent living with his grandfather. He was a miner, but being unable to find work locally he moved to Tavistock in Devon where, by his and his biographer's admission he 'allowed his soul to be stained by vile sins.' He lodged in a tavern and in his own words 'after being absent from my native county for seven years, I returned a drunkard.'

His return coincided with his transformation. He gave up drinking and very soon was proclaiming himself 'the King's Son.' God had entered his life and would remain his guiding influence for the rest of his days. Some stories suggest that his conversion was hastened by a near miss when the roof of the mine he was working in collapsed and he was nearly killed. Seeing visions of Hell before him, he called out to God and was saved to carry on His work. Others tell that he was given a book entitled *Visions of Heaven and Hell* by John Bunyan and that was the influence which changed him. Whatever the reason for this former drunken miner undergoing such a sudden and dramatic change, he soon became as passionate a Methodist Minister as any who have trod that path before or since. He not only preached but helped, with his own hands, to build the very buildings in which he gave his sermons with vigour sufficient to shake the very rafters. Billy Bray married a distant cousin, Susannah, and they had five children. He is perhaps best summed up by a friend and contemporary, Reverend William Haslam, a man whose story is equally worthy of reading.

Although their brand of faith may have been different in some ways, and indeed many aspects of their lives were very different, both were captured by their faith in very dramatic fashion. William Haslam was vicar of Baldhu Church when Billy Bray was preaching his fiery brand of the Methodist faith in the same area and where, less than half a mile from the church, Billy built his famous Three Eyes Chapel on Kerley Downs, still used to this day for worship. The two men met and discussed, even argued, about their sometimes different or conflicting beliefs but over time they became firm friends. Haslam says in his autobiographical work, *Leaves from my Notebook*:

My old friend Billy Bray of Cornwall was a right down happy soul. He was always singing and rejoicing, not only in voice but in every gesture of his body. He had a theory that if he praised God with his mouth only, at the Resurrection he would be like those things on the

The inscription on Billy Bray's memorial in Baldhu Churchyard sums up his life.

tombstones, all mouth and wings. If he clapped with his hands, he would rise with a pair of hands, but what a funny thing Billy Bray would be with mouth and hands! But if he danced on his feet, then he would rise complete, and men would see what the dear Lord could make of poor Billy Bray. There was some inkling of truth in this quaint and facetious saying. The good fellow intended to give himself up entirely to the Lord for ever, and he had done it. Miss Havergal expressed a like sentiment in more civilised language in her hymn:

Take my life and let it be,
Consecrated, Lord, to Thee.

But what of other bearers of the Bray name? There is a Bray family of Treswithian, Camborne, whose family line appears in J. L. Vivian's *Visitations of the County of Cornwall*, published in 1887. The family line begins with William Bray and Margery who had two sons, John, 1546–1601 and Henry, who married Margery, daughter of Walter Borlassy or Borlase of Newlyn, a family name we have looked at previously. Another Bray line which Vivian records is based in St Cleer, in north Cornwall, again as far back as the reign of Henry VIII when Ingerlam de Bray (the French connection?) owned Roscradek in St Cleer parish. Interestingly this Bray family married into the Tubb family of Gwennap parish and brought the name to the west of the county – the very same area as gave us Billy Bray. There was also a William Bray, noted seventeenth-century Church of England clergyman, and another William Bray, historian and writer on antiquities at the turn of the eighteenth and nineteenth centuries. Many Cornish Bray families were among the thousands who left these shores for a new life in other parts of the world. Sir John Cox Bray, nineteenth-century Australian legal practitioner and politician who rose to be premier of South Australia, was the son of an English bootmaker, Thomas Cox Bray. To link us neatly back to a previous name we have explored, that of Argal, the English-born American composer, John Bray wrote his opera *The Indian Princess* in 1808, just three years after settling in his adopted country. The opera tells the story of Captain John Smith and his love for the Indian princess Pocahontas, who later married John Rolfe and came with him to England.

The Bray name has featured in the Olympic Games with John Bray winning a bronze medal in athletics for America in 1900 and, more recently, Trent Bray representing New Zealand in the 1996 swimming events. Quite probably all can track their origins back to Cornwall, as it

Left: Billy Bray's memorial, Baldhu Churchyard.

Below: Billy Bray's 'Three Eyes Chapel' on Kerley Downs, near Chacewater, which is still in use today.

is without doubt one of those names not to be found elsewhere without some kind of Cornish connection in a previous generation.

BUZZA

A name probably derived from *bossow,* meaning 'dwelling', but here again there are various possibilities, some again involving foreigners, this time the Huguenots, or fifteenth-century French *Harquebuse* guns, or even from the Italian *Buzzacarina,* meaning 'ship builder'. My feeling is that if it were introduced by some French or Italian influences then it would not be as uniquely Cornish as it is. Of 105 Buzza names on the 1861 census, 102 are in Cornwall. The other three are a Cornish mariner, at sea at the time of the census, and a young married woman and her child living in London with her parents. Her husband was John Buzza, a carpenter originally from Cornwall. What further evidence is needed to call this name truly Cornish?

CARBIS

Another name of uncertain origins. Most suggest it is from *Car Pons* meaning 'cart bridge'. Others suggest it may have its origins in 'camp on a bridge' or even 'paved causeway', whilst *History of the British Isles* by C. L. Estrange Owen suggests the origin of the first part is *Kar* meaning 'rock'. It is generally agreed that 'rock' is *Carrek* in the Celtic tongue, so perhaps one of the suggestions about a place where carts cross bridges or folk are to be found camping on bridges or paved causeways across a river may be true after all. Another source suggests a link with the town of Carbes in southern France, whilst yet another suggestion is that the name dates back even further and that it is in some way connected to Carthage, founded by the Phoenicians several hundred years BC, who were known to trade along the eastern seaboard of the Atlantic as far as Cornwall. One of their trading points may have been Carbis Bay, near St Ives, close to where alluvial tin washes down the Red River at Gwithian. Quite possible, for although Carbis Bay is a modern name for the old Cornish place name of Porthreptor, there is a Carbons Farm noted in the area at least as far back as the sixteenth century. Whatever the origin, its earliest recorded mention in Cornwall appears to be in the Looe area around 1300 and thereafter its spread became countywide, reaching as far west as the mines of St Just in Penwith.

Despite uncertain origins, one thing for certain is that around 90 per cent of the nation's bearers of the name are to be found in Cornwall at the time of the 1861 census, and of those who are elsewhere, some give Cornish locations as their birth place. One of these is James Carbis, a retired attorney, originally from St Austell who is living near Kingsbridge in Devon with family members. He died there in 1866 at the age of sixty-two. His family were in the legal profession for two or three generations at least and his father, Nicholas, is to be found as a scrivener, or writer of deeds, for many of Cornwall's landed gentry of the late eighteenth and early nineteenth centuries. By complete contrast, another Nicholas Carbis is to be found on various records for the parish of Gwennap near Redruth as a ginger beer manufacturer, a trade he followed there for at least thirty years. Other Carbis names are associated with a wide variety of trades, including John Carbis, coach maker of Penzance, whose business was located at Parade Passage for well over forty years and whose family had roots in the village of Gulval going back several generations. Another John Carbis was parish clerk in Gulval for many years in the early nineteenth century. The Carbis families around the Redruth, Truro and Liskeard areas are mainly associated with mining and there is evidence that some Carbis men have already left these shores for foreign parts with Mary, the wife of Thomas Carbis of St Columb shown on census records as 'wife of miner abroad', a sure indication that we are looking at a time when Cornwall's miners were having to go far away to find work for themselves.

CARLYON

This is a name whose origins appear to be connected with the Celtic for 'earthwork' or 'hill fort'. There is also a suggestion that it may have been first used in Roman times and mean camp of the (Roman) legion. It is a name found across Cornwall, but whereas the Carlyon families of the Helston area seem to be mainly farming folk, those from other parts of the county seem to have professions such as teacher, solicitor, churchman and even widow of a police inspector. To us today, the name is clearly associated with Carlyon Bay and the St Austell area and it is here at Tregrehan, on the outskirts of St Austell, that the Carlyon family have had their estate since 1565. Like many of Cornwall's oldest and wealthiest families, the Carlyon family were great plant hunters and creators of great gardens. The garden at Tregrehan dates back to the 1730s when Philip Carlyon, a successful mining man and keen gardener, was planting woodlands and selling trees. Later generations included William Carlyon who sadly suffered from dementia in his final years and upon his death his brother, Colonel Edward Carlyon, took on Tregrehan. Through the 1840s he remodelled parts of the garden, added a very large greenhouse and employed the services of William Nesfield, a noted landscape architect whose other commissions had included Regents Park, St James Park and Kew Gardens. Plants were brought from all corners of the world, some by those most noted of Cornish plant collectors William and Thomas Lobb, who collected specimens on behalf of James Veitch & Son. William handed on the estate to another Thomas Carlyon and improvements continued. In 1914, Tregrehan was described by Professor Charles Sprague Sargent, Director of the Arnold Arboretum at Harvard University, as 'the best thing of its kind in the world'. Two years later, in 1916, the prolific horticultural writer W. J. Bean wrote on 'the Arboretum of Tregrehan'. Right down to this day the gardens are a picture and attract many visitors to admire the work of the Carlyon family down many generations.

The Carlyon name has also been closely associated with the church. Edward Carylon of Truro was Rector of Dibden on the edge of the New Forest in Hampshire for many years in the mid-nineteenth century, whilst Thomas Stackhouse Carlyon, also originally from Truro, became Rector of Glenfield in Leicestershire. He was the son of Dr Clement Carlyon, a noted physician in Truro who did much to improve the general sanitary conditions of the town. He described them as 'dirty, miserably narrow, ill-contrived and ill-ventilated'. He was Mayor of Truro in 1824 and again from 1844 to 1847. He helped to form the Board of Health and an Improvements Commission in 1835. Over the next few years under his guidance, a wide ranging scheme to improve the overall cleanliness and health of Truro was brought in. It even extended to the issue of whitewash and brushes for tenants and owners to paint their houses. Perhaps the most long-lasting improvement made at this time was a system of leats, designed to help cleanse the streets. This system is still in operation today, taking water from the river and running through a complex system of pipes, drains and culverts through the town.

The name of Carlyon has also been associated with the legal profession for many generations in Cornwall. The 1935 *Who's Who of Cornwall* gives us one example, Edmund Laurence Carlyon, J. P., Solicitor, Trevaunance, Truro. Born in 1863 in Stoodley, Devon, he was the son of the late Frederick Carlyon, M. A. Cantab. Educated in Felsted, Essex, in 1894 he married Margaret, daughter of the late James Jago M. D. F. R. S. In his spare time, he was a keen golfer.

The name of Carlyon also has a long and distinguished association with the post of County Coroner.

CARNE

—◦◦◦—

The next name we look at has its origins firmly set in the Celtic language. It is derived from *Carn,* meaning 'rock pile' and we have many examples in place names across Cornwall from Carn Galva in the far west, through Carn Brea overlooking Camborne and Redruth, to Carn Eglos in the Bodmin area. Its distribution as a family name is equally wide, from St Buryan in the west to St Germans in the east.

One of the most famous Carne families in Cornwall in the late eighteenth and early nineteenth centuries was that of William Carne, a banker from Penzance. He it was who joined with Messrs Boase and Batten to form Batten, Carne & Boase, the bankers who we met previously under the section on the Boase name. William's son Joseph became a partner in 1823 and the name changed to Batten, Carne & Carne. When Joseph died in 1858 his daughter Elizabeth Catherine Thomas Carne became the third generation of the Carne family to have an interest in the business. It was quite unusual at the time for a lady to take such an active part in business as did Elizabeth Carne. But that was not the only interest of this particular Carne family. Before becoming a partner in the banking business, Joseph Carne, William's eldest son, born in 1782, had already carved a notable career as a geologist. His first employment was as manager of the Cornish Cooper

Company's smelting works at Hayle, and this served to give him access to specimens of rock from all over west Cornwall, a continuation of a boyhood leisure activity. His interest was well known to local miners, as was the fact that he was willing to buy unusual rock specimens for a few pence, a welcome bonus to the often poor wages of the miner.

In various papers from around 1816 he wrote on the subject of Cornish minerals for the Royal Geological Society of Cornwall and became quite an authority on his subject. Joseph Carne was elected as a fellow of the Royal Society in 1818. He also wrote on other matters, ranging from the history of copper mining in Cornwall to the formation of the sand dunes to be found on Cornwall's north coast in the area around Perranporth. His famous mineral collection was taken on in later years by his grandson, Charles Campbell Ross. Born in London, Ross became a partner in the Carne family banking business in Penzance and also represented the St Ives Division as Member of Parliament. His family home was in Penzance and is now the Morrab Library and Gardens. The Ross Bridge in Penzance, built in 1881, is named after Charles Campbell Ross, who was Mayor of the town at the time. He served in that office five times from 1877-1883.

Like her father before her, Elizabeth Catherine Thomas Carne had an active interest in the minerals and geology of west Cornwall. She was elected a member of the Royal Geological Society of Cornwall, a rare honour for a woman of her time. With the help of the considerable wealth she inherited on the death of her father in 1858 she not only travelled extensively in Europe but also wrote about her travels. She contributed articles regularly to the *London Quarterly Review* as well as writing several books, one of which *Three Months Rest at Pau in the Winter and Spring of 1859,* she wrote under the unusual pseudonym of John Altrayd Wittitterly. *Country Towns and the place they fill in Modern Civilisation* followed in 1868 with *England's Three Wants* and *The Realm of Truth* shortly afterwards. Heady stuff for a Victorian lady! Back in Penzance she was a generous benefactor to local schools. She also paid for the building of a museum to house the extensive family mineral collection and other exhibits.

Yet another member of this Carne dynasty was John Carne, born in 1789, son of William and younger brother to Joseph, who we have met. John was originally destined to follow in his father's footsteps in the banking world but a short spell in this life convinced them both that his talents lay elsewhere. He travelled extensively, mostly to centres of ancient civilisations and religion such as Constantinople,

Greece, Egypt and Palestine. Whilst travelling in Palestine he was taken prisoner for a short while by Bedouin tribesmen, but was released unharmed. He wrote about his travels in a series of articles in the *New Monthly Magazine* and later reproduced these letters in book form under the title *Letters from the East*. His work received acclaim from such noteworthy names as Sir Walter Scott, perhaps the most well known author of his generation and William Jerdan, another Scotsman who was a noted political and travel writer of his time. Carne's *Letters from the East* detailing his travels in Eastern Europe and beyond was followed by his *Tales of the West* in 1828. This was a volume set much closer to home, with sections on the Lizard Peninsula, Newlyn and local legend, for John Carne was also a noted teller of tales as well as an exceptional writer of fact gleaned from his travels. Sadly, John Carne's health deteriorated in his early forties and he died in Madron at the age of fifty-five in 1844. He is buried in Gulval churchyard, as are other members of this quite unique Cornish family.

It seems that an interest in geology followed the Carne family to the other side of the world. Joseph Edmund Carne was born in 1855 in New South Wales, Australia, and participated in the Geological Survey of New South Wales from 1879 to 1883, alongside Charles Smith Wilkinson, an English-born geologist whose family had close connections to George Stephenson, the railway pioneer. Joseph Carne also travelled extensively in the southern hemisphere and the Carne River in Papua New Guinea is named after him. He became assistant government geologist in 1902 and head of that department from 1916 until his retirement in 1919. Thomas Carne's grandfather was Cornish-born Lieutenant Thomas Carne, related to the Carne banking family, who had gone to Australia in 1814 with the 46th (South Devon) Regiment of Foot.

CARTHEW

—*∿∿*—

From the Celtic *Car du*, meaning 'black fort' this is again a place name found across Cornwall as well as a family name. The village of Carthew, just outside St Austell, now houses the county's china clay museum at Wheal Martin, and it is the family name of Carthew which is very much associated with the expansion of the early china clay industry. In 1782, local man John Carthew formed a partnership with the potter Josiah Wedgwood and created the Cornwall China Clay Company. Within a few years large open cast workings were springing up all over the area, leaving behind their spoil heaps, known locally as the Cornish Alps. John Carthew's family had been in the area for many generations, at least as far back as the earliest surviving church records in the seventeenth century. His son, again named John, moved to Truro and became a printer by trade. There is a family connection here to the name of Thomas Gillett, who was long-time editor of the *West Briton* newspaper.

CAUSLEY

Found more commonly in Cornwall as Casley, I can offer no definite meaning to this name. Some sources give it as a derivation of *Caslys,* and may have originally meant 'clearing in the wood'. Others are not so sure, its origins then are perhaps best said to be lost in the mists of time.

One true Cornish bearer of the name certainly not lost in the mists of time is the poet, Charles Causley, born in Launceston in 1917. His early years were filled with sadness and poverty. His father died when he was still just a boy, having suffered for many years the ill effects of fighting in the trenches of the First World War. Money was always short and after his father's death, Charles was brought up by his widowed mother. He began his working career as a clerk in a builder's office. By his teenage years he had already written a play as well as poetry and was an accomplished piano player. He saw active service for his country in the Navy throughout the Second World War and later wrote about his experiences and some of the many and varied characters he met in a collection of poems under the title *Farewell Aggie Weston* and a book of short stories entitled *Hands to Dance,* published in 1951. He also wrote children's stories and poetry. He took a teacher training course after the war and once qualified, returned to his home town of Launceston where he taught until his retirement. He never married and enjoyed living a very quiet life, not seeking the limelight, but his poetry brought him both local and national recognition. He was awarded the Queen's Gold Medal for Poetry in 1967 and became a CBE in 1986. Charles Causley died at the age of eighty-six on 4 November 2003 and was laid to rest beside his mother in the churchyard of St Thomas, Launceston, his lifelong home town.

The spelling interpretation of Causley is, however, found far more in Devon than in Cornwall, and is particularly prevalent in the Newton Abbot area. The Cornish Casley variation is found exclusively in the west of the county. In fact, it can safely be said that as many as 90 per cent of Casley families were originally miners in St Just in Penwith. The one 1861 Casley family who have 'escaped' from this enclave have even then only gone about twenty miles up the road as far as Crowan, where the head of the family, John Casley, is working as a blacksmith. Oh, but even he gives his place of birth as St Just!

Some names we have met and will meet in future pages have been around for countless generations and yet stay restricted to one location, whereas others are to be found all over Cornwall. We shall discuss possible reasons for this a little later but Casley is one such name which has been around certainly as far back as the marriage of William Casely, as it is spelt at the time, and Grace Williams in St Just in Penwith on 22 October 1615.

Staying in the west of Cornwall, the name of Casley also has close associations with cricket, in particular Mullion Cricket Club. Clifford Casley was a stalwart of that club for many seasons and also played for Cornwall. The family name is still to be found today in the club's scorebooks.

CHEGWIN

—◈—

Chegwin, Chirgwin and Chegwidden seem to be the same name. According to most sources they are all derived from *Chy* or *Che* for 'cottage' or 'house' with *gwin, gwyn or gwidn* meaning 'white' or 'light-coloured'. There is also a suggestion that *gwyns* meaning 'wind' may play a part in the derivation of the name, so again we have a divergence of opinion, on which I am not about to challenge or take sides. One thing which is safe to say is that very few bearers of these names are to be found outside Cornwall and so the names are truly Cornish, whichever original meaning you decide upon.

The name is quite common in and around many of Cornwall's mining areas, such as Gwennap, Redruth and Wendron and one interesting family on the census of 1861 is that of Peter Chegwidden, a gunpowder manufacturer living with his wife and family in Ponsanooth. He was in this trade all his life, first of all from premises in Truro and later moving to Ponsanooth, where he worked for the Kennal Vale Gunpowder Company. His son, also named Peter, followed in his father's footsteps and worked at Kennal Vale too. In addition to being the manufacturers of gunpowder, which was used extensively in the local mines before the days of the more reliable dynamite and gelignite, some family members were also coopers, makers of the barrels in which the gunpowder was stored and transported. A self-contained family business!

Today Kennal Vale echoes not to the sound of the gunpowder industry but to the sights and sounds of a nature reserve, along whose streams and charming walks can still be seem some of the relics of its industrial past.

CHENOWETH

No less a scholar than A.L. Rowse writes in his book, *The Cornish in America,* 'the name is a pure Cornish name, meaning new house, and could be nothing else.' Alfred Leslie Rowse was born in 1903 and wrote more about Cornwall and the Cornish and has had more written about him than most Cornishmen who ever lived. I am not about to disagree in any way with one of Cornwall's most respected sons on the meaning of this name. There is a Chenoweth Family Association based in America, books have been written about the family's history including *The History of the Chenoweth family* and *The Chenoweth family in America* and family reunions are a regular feature of Chenoweth life. But when did the name first appear and where? Like so many it is obviously very old and from the Cornish Celtic tongue and so its true origins may never be known. Neither may the first bearer of the name who lived in the 'new house', but down the centuries, many Chenoweth family members have left their mark in a variety of ways.

Our benchmark, the 1861 census, actually lists more folk with the variation Chynoweth than the original Chenoweth and in total there are no more than 200 bearers of both the variations of the name across the county. Although truly Cornish, it only just scrapes in to the top 150 most common names in the county at that time. Half of the

Chynoweth spelling and over a third of the Chenoweth variation are in the Truro area. There are a small number as far east as Camelford and one Camelford Chenoweth family who have moved to Liskeard, but in the main the name is found in and around Truro, Redruth and the Helston area. There are a lot of miners from our great Cornish mining parishes like Kenwyn, Illogan and St Agnes in the mix, and this is one reason why the name is now found all across America, as this was a favourite destination for Cornish mining families when our mines here suffered severe decline in the later decades of the nineteenth century.

Perhaps one of the best known of the early American Chenoweth names was Lemuel Chenoweth. He was born in 1811 in West Virginia, the son of John and Mary. He grew to be a noted architect and bridge builder and one shining example of his work still remains a modern day part of the US Federal Highway system. The 285ft long Phillipi Covered Bridge on US Route 250 across the Tygart Valley River was built in 1852, and despite being nearly destroyed by the ravages of civil war and a couple of major fires, it remains intact and looking much as it did over 150 years ago. It is the site of what most agree was the first land battle of the American Civil War in June 1861 and was used as a barracks by Union troops. Local legend also says that Abraham Lincoln met Jefferson Davis on the bridge towards the end of the American Civil War to begin peace negotiations. Lemuel and his brother Eli built over twenty bridges on major highway routes across this part of America but sadly most are now long gone, replaced in most cases by more modern structures.

But what of some of the Chenoweth families who stayed here in Cornwall? Some it seems were rather less than law abiding. A quick look at Quarter Sessions records for the early years of the nineteenth century will see Michael Chenoweth imprisoned for deserting his wife and family, William Chenoweth summoned for being the father of an illegitimate child, and Richard Chenoweth also in the same situation 'to remain in custody until the child is born.' One Thomas Chenoweth was also before the Magistrates Court for assault on a young lady 'intending carnal knowledge.' But not all were of bad character and even those listed above I suspect were normally honest working men, digging a living out of Cornwall's mines and fields.

Thomas Chenoweth, born in St Just in Roseland in 1828, is to be found by 1841 living with his widowed mother, Jane. He became a blacksmith by trade and passed this skill on to at least two of his sons. One of these, Walter, was village blacksmith in Veryan for well over thirty years. Another son, Richard, also followed this trade. He went for some years to South Africa where he married and had three children before returning to Cornwall towards the end of the 1880s.

Like so many of the names we are looking at, some of the bearers made their fame and fortune and some have simply done what needed to be done to earn a living and raise the next generation.

COAD

Possibly derived from *coth* meaning 'old' or perhaps *cos* meaning 'wood'. But then again, there is a suggestion from the Coad One Name Study group, who should know about these things, which suggests that the name was first found around 1600 in the Exeter area of Devon, that it soon spread to Cornwall, and that it is a variant of Cowde or Coard, and that both of these are shortened forms of Cowherd. So perhaps we have old cows living in a wooded area? Again, opinion is divided on the origin of the name. Modern day variants include Coade, Code, Cood and Coode.

Cornwall's proportion of the national Coad family name is nearly 60 per cent in the 1861 census with Devon having a further 12 per cent, almost all of whom are close to the Cornwall border - places like Plymouth and Tavistock being prominent - so even those in Devon are almost in Cornwall. There are also Cornish and Devonshire Coad families working away from their native counties in places like London, so add all these together and it can be said to be a true west country name, if not exclusively Cornish.

One noteworthy Cornish nineteenth-century bearer of the Coad name was Robert Coad, born in 1778, son of Robert and Rebecca Coad from Menheniot. He became a noted engineer and surveyor. Perhaps his greatest achievement was the construction of the Liskeard to Looe canal. Cornwall is not normally noted as suitable for canals, it is too hilly, but a few were built here between Liskeard and Looe, also at Bude in the north of Cornwall and a few other locations, mainly for use to carry agricultural cargoes and ore from the mines to sea ports. First proposed as far back as 1777, the Liskeard to Looe canal was surveyed but not then built, and the idea fell out of fashion for almost fifty years until 1824 when the Liskeard and Looe Union Canal Act was passed. Construction began in 1825 and the canal was opened in 1827, although it was not fully completed until 1830 on a six mile route with twenty-four locks. Its main engineers and surveyors were Robert Coad, James Green and Richard Retallick. Its heyday was from the 1830s to the 1850s, during which time quays at Moorswater on the outskirts of Liskeard were buzzing with activity. Although agricultural cargoes such as limestone, sand and manure were all listed on the tariff chart for the canal, the main cargo was ore from the extremely productive South Caradon, West Caradon, Marke Valley and Phoenix mines, all great producers of copper ore in their time. Ore would be taken down to the sea at Looe for export, with coal and timber brought back up the canal for onward distribution to the mines further inland around Minions and St Cleer. A spider's web of branches soon developed from the many mines in the area, as well as from the granite works around the Cheesewring and Kilmar Tor, all leading down from the heights of Bodmin Moor to Liskeard and then by canal to Looe. With the coming of the railway, canal traffic became rail traffic and the canal route formed the basis of the rail route between Liskeard and Looe. Strangely, it operated for a further thirty years still under the Liskeard and Looe Union Canal name but as a rail link, finally becoming the Great Western Railway branch line in 1909. All that remains of these once great mines are the silent chimney stacks, reminders of a bygone age of prosperity for the area. Although the cargoes of copper ore, granite and even limestone and manure for the farmers are a thing of the distant past, the rail line still operates to this day, mainly on the former canal route between the two towns.

One of Robert Coad's sons, John, born in 1824, became a solicitor and deputy coroner and ran his business from Liskeard. The family name, with some spelling variations, is still associated with the legal profession to this day in Cornwall.

COLENSO

—⁓—

Another name originating in the Celtic tongue, this time in three parts, *Ke* or *Cae* meaning 'hedge', *lyn,* meaning 'pool' and *dhu,* meaning 'black' giving us 'the black hedged pool', or 'a pool of dark peaty water surrounded by a hedge'.

It is one of our selection of names which can truly be said to be quite uniquely Cornish. Of all the Colenso families on the 1861 census, only a small handful are not in Cornwall and without exception those who have moved from their native county give Cornish places of birth. One family has moved to Wolverhampton where the head of the household, William Colenso, originally from Crowan, is a corporal in the local police force. Emily Colenso from Cornwall is a school teacher in Plymouth, whilst William Colenso from Penzance is now a bootmaker in the Paddington area of London. These, and a couple of servant girls who have also gone off to London to seek their fortune, make up the whole Colenso contingent outside Cornwall.

Of those within the county, they are mainly to be found in the west, particularly around Madron and Penzance where most have individual trades such as cordwainer, carpenter, blacksmith, mason and painter. A little further east around Crowan and Breage, the Colenso men are mainly miners.

Perhaps the best known Colenso to make his name outside Cornwall was John William Colenso, born in Pentewan, St Austell in 1814. His father, also John Colenso, was originally from Penzance and had moved to Pentewan where he ploughed all his money into a tin streaming works. Names such as Happy Union Tin Stream Works and Merry Meeting suggest an idyllic scene, but sadly the Colenso family fortune was literally washed away when the works were destroyed by the sea. This left John Colenso unable to send his very promising son to university, but John junior was not to be denied and a combination of working in his spare time and a small loan from family enabled him to study at St John's, Cambridge. In 1836 he was Second Wrangler at Cambridge, a Wrangler being the term used to describe one who has completed his third year Mathematics Tripos with Honours. The highest award was Senior Wrangler, followed by Second Wrangler. The Cornish mathematician and astronomer, John Couch Adams, had the honour of Senior Wrangler at Cambridge a little later in 1839, and both men followed in the footsteps of Henry Martyn from Truro, who had been Senior Wrangler some years before and who went on to make his name as a linguist and missionary. Among many other achievements, he translated the Psalms into Persian and the Book of Common Prayer into Urdu. So Colenso's achievement in coming second in a prize list topped by these two other famous Cornishmen in their time was quite outstanding.

John Colenso was briefly maths tutor at Harrow School. At the time, Harrow was not attracting too many of the brightest and best and this, together with a devastating fire in which he lost most of his possessions, left Colenso again in debt. He wrote reference manuals on algebra and arithmetic in the early 1840s and sold these to publishers to help pay his debts. He later joined the church and became Rector of Forncett St Mary in Norfolk in 1846, and in 1853 he went to South Africa as the first Bishop of Natal. He continued his writing and one of his early works in South Africa was an English to Zulu dictionary. Soon he was translating the New Testament into the Zulu language and encouraging the native Zulus to write their own accounts of their history and their wars. He became quite a controversial character within church circles. He questioned many parts of the Old Testament, especially some of the stories in the Pentateuch, suggesting for example that the story of Noah's Ark could not be taken literally and historically as fact and that the factual and historical nature of many other stories within the first few books of the Old Testament had to be questioned. This led him into direct conflict with the leaders of the Church of England whose basic beliefs still lay in Genesis. All this and Darwin too, it was certainly 'light the blue touch paper and stand back' time in the evolution of scientific understanding of the origins of the human species.

COMBELLACK

This is another name exclusive to Cornwall at the time of the 1861 census. Its meaning though is again open to interpretation. The *Com* is generally thought to be derived from *Carn* meaning 'rock pile' but the second part could be from *Belek,* which is Breton for 'priest' or possibly *pellek,* meaning 'rounded'. So 'priest's rock pile' or 'rounded rock pile', take your pick.

If you threw a large nineteenth-century blanket over the three parishes of Gwennap, Wendron and Constantine you would cover almost all of the Cornish Combellack clan and most are engaged in mining. At this time, the vast majority of miners in Cornwall were digging ore from many fathoms underground, but there was still some alluvial tin streaming activity in parts of the county. Streaming for ore in Cornwall was a very ancient process with roots dating back to the pre-Christian era. It is essentially the recovery of particles of ore by washing it out of water courses which have run through underground mineral seams. A small section of water course would be dammed, and over a period of time an alluvial sediment deposit would be trapped behind this dam. The heavier mineral deposits would sink into the alluvial mud behind the dam and this muddy substance would then be washed and sifted to extract the valuable metals.

Even in Victorian times there were areas where alluvial tin streaming was still an important source of mineral wealth and one of these areas was Wendron parish. The Cober River flows through this area. Its source is a little further inland in the mineral rich high ground around Nine Maidens Downs in the Praze and Four Lanes area just on the south side of the ridge. This also provides the source of the Red River, which flows to the north coast and which is so named because of the colouration of its waters, caused by alluvial mineral deposits. The Cober flows from underground springs down to eventually meet the sea at Loe Bar, and as it does so it gathers mineral deposits from deep underground and these were captured by the tin streamers of Wendron. One family name very closely associated with tin streaming in Wendron parish was the name of Combellack. Records for the late 1830s show as many as five Combellack families relying on tin streaming for a living. Life was hard for these tin streamers, just as hard as for the miners underground in many ways. They were almost constantly wading around the muddy sediment from which they extracted the particles of tin ore and consequently suffered ill health from being wet and cold much of the time.

CRAGO

If you are a Crago or have Crago in your family, then you are most certainly of Cornish origins, for here again we have a name which is to be found almost exclusively in Cornwall in the mid-nineteenth century. To be more specific than that, it is a name where some 80 per cent or more can trace their ancestry to the Liskeard area with the parishes of St Keyne, St Pinnock and Braddock, or Broadoak as it used to be, being to the fore. The name derives from *Crugyow,* meaning 'mounds' or 'barrows', as in ancient burial grounds, so here again a question. Why, when these ancient burial mounds occur throughout

Cornwall, is a family name apparently linked to them found mainly in such a small part of the county?

I grant you that there are Crago families to be found in other parts of Cornwall, but with very few exceptions, all birth places lead back to within a few miles of Liskeard. Interestingly there is a small branch of the family with an 'e' added to the end making Cragoe, to be found in and around Manaccan on the Helford River. It would seem that this is not just an enumerator's error or misinterpretation of spelling, as it appears in other census records and in the parish registers down several generations. There seems no logical reason for a connection between a mainly farming family name in and around Liskeard and a small number with the same name who have water-borne trades in a completely different part of the county, but that is the beauty and the mystery of family history research.

CREBO

Most agree that the origins of this name are to be found in the Celtic word *Crybow*, meaning 'ridge' or 'crest of a hill'. However a second opinion is that it is from *Crebon*, meaning 'wrinkled' or 'withered'. It is again a name found with differing spellings in different parts of Cornwall. If you are a Creba you are more likely to be from the St Austell area, whereas Crebo is found further west around Truro and down as far as Penzance. Both can be said to be Cornish as there are very few elsewhere in the country. The name can be found in some of the oldest parish registers in Cornwall and probably predates these by many generations. Again, place names featuring the same name are to be found. Polcrebo in Crowan parish dates from at least as far back as 1327 when it is found as Polcrebon, later becoming Polcrybowe. Perhaps this is the true home of the name, it certainly seemed so to Richard R. Blewett when he analysed the 1953 electoral registers, which we have referred to in our introduction.

CURNOW

Who are these people called Curnow or Kernow? A simple enough question you may think. They are named after this wonderful county we call Cornwall; they are the true Cornish. But consider this. Where did they come from and are they all west of that traditional border between Cornwall and England, the River Tamar?

In one of his articles on Cornish surnames, Richard R. Blewett begins with two Shakespearean quotes:

> The merciless MacDonwald of Kerns and Gallowglasses is supplied.
> *Macbeth*

> Now for our Irish Warres we must supplant those rug-headed Kernes.
> *Richard II*

Gallowglasses were mercenary warriors once based in the Western Isles of Scotland who were originally of Gaelic and Nordic descent.

Kern is an English adaptation of the Irish word *ceithern* or *ceatharn* meaning 'a band of foot soldiers'. Mr Blewett goes on to explain that 'the Celtic method of forming the plural was the addition of "ow" to the singular', and so we arrive at Kernow.

But do we have exclusive right to this name here west of the Tamar? The answer to that, it seems, is no. Consider the ancient Cornovii, a Celtic tribe who inhabited this south western peninsula of what we now know as England during a period ranging from the Iron Age through to the post-Roman period. As far back as the year AD 700, there is written evidence for walled forts of the Cornovii in this part of the world.

According to most sources, the Cornovii were probably a branch of the Dumnonii tribe whose lands included the modern day Cornwall, Devon and west Somerset. The name Cornubia is also one which is in use for their territory by AD 700, the meaning of this being 'people of the horn shaped peninsula', so the Tamar is a relatively modern boundary for the Kerns or Cornish. Indeed boundary changes in Victorian and even more modern times have changed some parishes from being in Cornwall to Devon and back again. There is a house in Kingsand on the Rame Peninsula, now wholly in Cornwall, but which still shows a vertical divide, with apparently half the house being in Cornwall and half in Devon. This is a remnant of the time before 1844 when Kingsand, once known as North Rockers, was in Devon and its immediate neighbour, Cawsand, or Turk Town, was in Cornwall, the 'boundary' then being a small stream behind the present day pub. This arrangement dates back to a time when it was decided that both sides of the strategically important Plymouth Sound should be administered by one authority to ensure consistency in running vital defences against the enemy. To add a little more to the melting pot of confusion, the name Cornovii is also to be found in ancient times describing peoples from the far north of Scotland, the area we now know as Caithness, and also around Gloucestershire and into Shropshire.

To return though to our main theme, 90 per cent of Curnows on the 1861 census are living in Cornwall, with others elsewhere giving Cornish birth places, so it is, for our purposes, a genuine Cornish family name. Nearly 70 per cent of the Curnow names are to be found in the west of the county around Penzance. Farming, mining and fishing appear to be the most common occupations, as you would expect in this part of Cornwall.

One story of interest with connections to the Curnow name is that of Catherine or Kate Curnow. She was born in Zennor and in 1870 married John Jenkin, a miner originally from Gwennap. The couple settled in St Ives and subsequently had several children, two of whom sadly died at an early age. One surviving son was Stephen Curnow Jenkin, born in 1880. He, like so many of his generation, emigrated and became a copper miner in Michigan, USA. He returned to St Ives to visit his parents in 1911 and his return trip was on the *Titanic*. He was tragically to be one of the 1,500 people who lost their lives when the ship hit an iceberg and sank. His body was never identified. The sad news was conveyed to his parents in St Ives and his name is etched with theirs on the family headstone in Barnoon cemetery. It is said that he had a premonition that his return trip to America would end in disaster and as a result he left some of his valued possessions with his parents in St Ives before embarking on the fateful voyage.

Other Curnow names are to be found scattered all over the world today, all of whom could probably trace their ancestry back to Cornwall. Thomas Allen Curnow CBE was one of New Zealand's foremost poets of the twentieth century, as well as being a lecturer in English at the University of Auckland. His father was an Anglican clergyman, Reverend Tremayne Curnow, a Cornish name if ever there was one, and the family were descended from early Cornish migrants. The Curnow family name is also represented in many other fields and is to be found all too often in the honoured ranks of those who have died in service of their country. The First World War claimed twenty-five men by the name of Curnow; nine of these were from Australia and one from Canada. A similar number are also to be found making the ultimate sacrifice in the Second World War.

DOWER

The origins of this name seem to be from the Celtic tongue, where *Dowr* means 'water'. So we have 'folk who live by the water'. However it is not exclusively a name found in Cornwall or even in Celtic parts of the country. Its mid-nineteenth century spread is quite wide and varied, from mid-Cornwall through Devon and Somerset on to Suffolk, Cambridgeshire and Lincolnshire in the east, up through the counties of Warwickshire and Leicestershire as far as Yorkshire and Lancashire in the north. Not all of them can claim direct Cornish ancestry either, so it is a name which probably, with centuries of use, has found itself all over England and Wales. Compare this then with other names we have seen where their origins appear to be equally as ancient but whose spread, even after many centuries of use, is confined to a few small parishes here in Cornwall. The reason for this? I have no definite idea but Dower, Dowry and Dower House all have connections with marriage, marital gifts and homes for widows granted from their late husband's estate, so perhaps the origins are different in other parts of England.

The name also occurs quite frequently in southern Ireland with the same spelling and in parts of northern France as Dauer, but here in Cornwall, the origins are almost certainly Celtic. Also in Cornwall there are several place names where Dower occurs; Tredower in St Martin in Meneage and St Minver parishes to name but two, and historically the name of Dyuer appears as a place name in Crowan parish as far back as 1317 and appears to be of the same origins, the name changed by the sixteenth century to Dowre. The Kenwyn river which passes through Truro was known until relatively recently as Dowr Ithy, meaning 'fragrant water', quite a misnomer when you consider that for many generations it formed part of the open sewer and drainage system for the town before the coming of extensive improvements in the nineteenth century.

A name then with attachments to rivers and place names as well as being quite a common family name.

EATHORNE

With or without the 'e' on the end, it is generally agreed that this name derives from *Eythyn,* meaning 'furze bush'. It is again one of those names which has been around for many millennia but has not spread very far. It is to be found mainly in the adjoining parishes of Wendron and Sithney with a few strays born in Falmouth. There is a place name of Eathorne in the parish of Mabe, near Penryn, which is a very ancient site. The name is noted in records of the Arundell family, one of Cornwall's wealthiest landowning families, as far back as 1449. The name appears later as Ethrorn in documents dating from 1492. The site is also known for the Eathorne Menhir, or 'standing stone'. This stone was the subject of some controversy a few years ago when the landowner pulled it out of the ground and dumped it in the hedge, as he was 'concerned by its Pagan origins'. It was stood upright again through the efforts of the Cornwall Archaeology unit but it was then covered in wire mesh by the landowner and fenced off. It gradually grew a covering of ivy and all but disappeared into the hedgerow. It sat there for another couple of years before the efforts of local people and readers of *Meyn Mamvro*, a magazine for devotees of the ancient stones and sacred sites of Cornwall, saw it retuned to its original site in the field away from the hedge where it has apparently stood since pre-Christian times.

One Eathorne not concerned with Pagan tradition was Paul Eathorne, born in Falmouth in 1802, of a family with firm roots in Helston. He became a shoemaker by trade but was also a well known Methodist Preacher in the Helston area in the mid-nineteenth century. He died at the age of eighty-four in 1886. His son, Edwin, had a greengrocer's business in Meneage Street, Helston, for many years but they were by no means the first Eathornes to have business connections with Helston. Records show William Eathorne, peruke maker (wig maker), had a thriving business in the town in the mid-eighteenth century which he inherited from his father, also William Eathorne. Sadly though, William's wigs either went out of fashion or he was not as good at his job as his father, for in 1774 he writes, 'My trade is not so profitable,' but implores his creditors to be patient saying, 'from your former activities to me, I dare say you will not be too quick upon me as long as you are satisfied that I mean fairly.'

John Eathorne, a brother to William junior, was also in business in Helston at the same time as a cordwainer, a leather worker or shoemaker, and this trade seems to have passed down the generations for more than a hundred years.

EDDY

If you have Eddy, Edy or Edey in your family tree then you are almost certain to track your ancestry back to west Cornwall. Over 70 per cent of the Eddy families listed on the 1861 census live in the Penzance registration district. To nail them down to an even smaller geographical area, the coastal mining parishes of St Just, Zennor, Sancreed, Towednack and Morvah are the heartland of the name. Eddy men were miners along this most rugged stretch of the Cornish coast, spending their lives many fathoms underground, working ore seams which very often stretched way out under the Atlantic Ocean. It was an extremely harsh environment and one which down the years is littered with tragic accidents. Mines such as Crowns and Wheal Owles, with their long-redundant engine houses clinging to the cliff-side near Botallack are stark reminders of these times and act as monuments to the sacrifice of the miners.

10 January 1893 is a date firmly fixed in Cornish mining history. It was the date when many miners died in the watery depths of Wheal Owles. As *The Cornishman* newspaper of 12 January reported:

> Nineteen men and a boy died in the watery darkness of Wheal Owles, at St Just in Penwith. A terrible roar was heard by the forty men and

boys working deep underground at Wheal Owles mine. On the morning of Tuesday 10 January the miners had broken through into the workings of the flooded neighbouring Wheal Drea. As the torrent rushed into Wheal Owles it pushed the air before it, creating a great wind which blew out all the lights, plunging the terrified miners into absolute darkness. Those working on the upper levels narrowly escaped with their lives. Nineteen men and a boy were never seen again. Their remains are still entombed in the flooded workings.

The bodies of those who died were never recovered and the mine never reopened. Such are the lasting memories of this tragic event that a centenary memorial service was held on 10 January 1993 in Chapel Street Methodist Church, St Just. At this service the names of those who perished were read out and, inevitably, there is an Eddy name amongst them. William Eddy, like all of those who died, left loved ones behind to mourn his passing.

Perhaps equally well known is the date 20 October 1919 when the man engine, a device used to raise and lower men to the working levels far below ground, failed at Levant mine, sending thirty-one miners to their death. Again the Eddy family name is amongst those killed. George Henry Eddy of Bosorne Road, St Just, has his name engraved on the memorial plaque which lists the names and addresses of all thirty-one men who died. He was of a mining family who could trace their ancestry and their connection to tin mining back many generations.

One Eddy of a previous generation fell foul of the law back in 1743 when he was committed for trial accused of 'stealing goods of John Borlase Esq. and others to the value of 10*d*'. William Eddy was found guilty and transported to America for seven years for his crimes.

Tragedy seems to follow the Eddy name wherever they go in the world. In his book *Cornishmen and Kiwis,* David Eddy writes of his Cornish ancestors from the area around Gulval, just to the east of Penzance. One of these was William Henry Eddy, whose ancestry has been tracked as far back as the early seventeenth century. He grew up in a small thatched cottage right next to the church in Gulval. The old cottage is now long gone but photographs of it remain. His father tragically died after being kicked by a horse when William was just eleven years old, and he and his four siblings were brought up by their widowed mother. William married Margaret Oats, also from a longstanding local family, in 1874 and on 26 September 1878, he and his cousin Richard Eddy, together with their wives and children, set off

Above: Crowns Mine engine house, standing perilously perched on the edge of the cliffs near Botallack.

Left: Crowns Mine, Botallack, one of many mines in this area where the search for ore took men way out under the Atlantic Ocean.

Those who lost their lives

Wheal Owles,
Monday, January 10, 1893.

Mark Taylor
John Taylor
Edward White
William Eddy
James Rowe
James Edwards
William Davey
William Roberts
Richard Williams
John Oats

Thomas Allen
William Thomas
John Grose
Thomas Grose
Lewis Blewett
Charles Thomas
James Williams
Peter Dale
James Thomas
Thomas Ellis

Above: The names of those tragically killed in two of Cornwall's worst ever mining accidents are inscribed on brass plaques in the Botallack Mining Museum.

Left and opposite: The now desolate Wheal Owles engine house stands on the cliffs near Botallack.

Levant Mine, scene of one of Cornwall's worst ever mining accident. On 19 October 1919, thirty-one men were killed when the Man Engine failed.

aboard the *Marlborough* for the other side of the world and settled near Christchurch, New Zealand. One of these children was William and Margaret's three month old baby, Margaret Ann. Sadly just four weeks into their journey, the baby died of what was called 'congestion of the brain' and, wrapped in sailcloth, was buried at sea. Their son, Alfred, then aged two, witnessed these events and later related the story that he was told that a little donkey had died and been buried. He did not realise at the time that it was his baby sister.

The *Marlborough* made good time on her voyage, reaching Lyttelton, New Zealand, in just seventy-eight days, one of the fastest passages on record for the journey. Three other passengers had died as well as the Eddy baby during the voyage. Even as they arrived, their troubles mounted as the whole ship's crew and passengers were quarantined following an outbreak of fever on board. Their lives in New Zealand were to take a turn for the better and William set up a market gardening business, selling his own produce as his mother had done back in Gulval. The couple had fourteen children, not including the baby who died on passage to New Zealand. The family business thrived and was soon selling across a wide area of the surrounding countryside. The family farm was known as Gulval Farm, in memory of his birthplace, and seems to have been mostly a happy and thriving family home and business.

A footnote on the *Marlborough*. She was a regular traveller on the route from England to New Zealand via Cape Horn. On her final fateful journey, she left Lyttelton on 11 January 1890 on a return trip to England and never arrived at her destination. She was last sighted a few days out of Lyttleton by a passing ship but her exact fate remains a mystery to this day. In 1913 the captain of another ship told a story of finding the wreck of the *Marlborough* near Cape Horn. His story contained several facts inconsistent with reality and as he had waited since 1899 to tell it, it was generally dismissed. Another apparent find of a sailcloth tent containing several skeletons and a small lifeboat with *Marlborough* on its side was also mainly dismissed. The fate of the ship was never truly resolved, but enquiries of other ships in the area at the time of her disappearance suggested unusual quantities of icebergs in latitudes where she was headed. The official enquiry into her loss concluded that the most likely explanation of her doom was that she hit an iceberg and sank to the bottom of the freezing Southern Ocean, taking all hands with her. There was no radio in those days to call for help, and probably a thousand miles from the nearest land in freezing and stormy waters, like so many others, she will lie forever in the cold ocean depths.

ENYS

In a paragraph in his *West Briton* article of 9 April 1959, Richard R. Blewett says:

> It is impossible to state a law by which historical roots can be reasoned by the size of a subnominal population. There are only three Trevanions left in Cornwall, thirteen Tremethicks, seven Trelawneys, two Tregennas and three Trefusis, but they have almost a thousand years of Cornish history behind them.

He could well have included the Enys name in this list. The 1861 census lists just one Enys family, living at Goonreeve, St Gluvias. There are but a small handful more who spell the name Ennis. However the name, which derives from the Celtic for 'a well watered place', has been here in Cornwall for up to a thousand years, perhaps more.

Robert de Enys lived at Enys, in St Gluvias parish during the reign of Edward 1 from 1272-1307 and some say that the name has been in this part of Cornwall since before the Norman Conquest of 1066, so it is certainly one of the oldest names in Cornwall. The estate at Enys also boasts the oldest garden in Cornwall.

The 1861 family is headed by John Samuel Enys, born in Worcestershire, who had inherited the Enys estate from his great uncle, Francis Enys, a lawyer who never married. With John Samuel in 1861 is his wife, Catherine, formerly Catherine Gilbert, daughter of Davies Gilbert, who was in his time a noted mathematician, and also a Member of Parliament and President of the Royal Society. There are three children of the Enys family here in 1861.

The first of these is Francis Gilbert Enys, born in 1836, who inherited the estate on his father's death in 1872. He was a local magistrate and holder of many other offices in Cornwall during his lifetime. The second, John Davies Enys, born in 1837, went to New Zealand for forty years with his younger brother, Charles.

The youngest in 1861 was Mary Anne Enys, born in 1839. She never married and died in 1914 at the age of seventy-five.

To cater for the needs of this small household of five there is a list of nine live-in servants; a coalman, coachman, groom, housekeeper, under-postman, cook, housemaid, kitchen maid and under housemaid. The Tudor house at Enys was destroyed by fire in the 1830s but rebuilt soon afterwards by John Samuel Enys to a design by architect Henry Harrison. With two of his sons, John Davies and Charles, away in New Zealand and sending back a host of plants for the garden, Enys soon became a sub-tropical garden paradise.

John Davies Enys studied botany, biology and geology whilst in New Zealand and also took an active part in local politics. He was elected to the Canterbury Provincial Council in 1870. Neither he nor his two brothers, who both died before him, married and so a continuous male line of succession dating back several hundred years was broken. With Mary Anne remaining a spinster all her life, it was only John Samuel and Catherine's older daughter, Jane, who were left to produce an heir to the estate. She had married Henry Rogers and so the Rogers name came to Enys. Sadly the next two generations did little to maintain or enhance the work of many generations before them and the property fell into a state of some disrepair. In 1980 Enys was inherited by Professor Gordon Leonard Rogers and he took an active interest again, setting up the Enys Trust in 2002 which has the task of carrying on centuries of work in the gardens for this and future generations.

As well as being landed gentry, generations of Enys family members have carved their names in the history books for other reasons. We have seen John and Charles in New Zealand, but before them another John Enys is worthy of mention. He was born in 1757, the youngest son of John and Lucy Enys, formerly Lucy Bassett, a family name we have already met. John was to be present at the birth of a nation, he had an Etonian education, befitting his status as the son of a wealthy family. He suffered from smallpox as a young man but happily recovered. His father purchased an Ensign's Commission for him in 1775 in the 29th Regiment of Foot and in March 1776, the regiment set sail for Quebec City. This was a time of the Revolutionary War in North America and John first saw action at the Battle of Trois Rivieres in June 1776, in which the Americans were defeated by General Carleton's British forces. John Enys was also present when Carleton's naval squadron defeated Benedict Arnold's American naval squadron at Valcour Island a few months later. American independence from British rule was finally agreed and John Enys returned to Cornwall, and was promoted to the rank of Captain. By 1794 he had been promoted to Major and saw action in the ensuing years of the Napoleonic Wars. He retired in 1800 after twenty-five years of service with the same regiment, by now with the rank of Lieutenant Colonel. He spent his final years in Bath where he died on 30 July 1818.

As we have seen, there may not have been many of them at any one time but the name of Enys fully deserves inclusion amongst the ranks in this book as one of the most distinguished names in the county for perhaps a thousand years.

EVA

From a name which has Celtic origins going back to the mists of time, we move to another Cornish name which is far more common than that of Enys, but whose origins are somewhat obscure. Mr Richard R. Blewett says of Eva:

The Cornish English dictionary gives 'eva' a verb, to drink, imbibe, sup…this evidence is very slender but it is all I can offer. I am uncertain of the Celtic origin of Eva.

G. Pawley White, in *A Handbook of Cornish Surnames,* suggests that the name is from the Celtic personal name *Hyviu.* An alternative suggestion is that the name is another which came across with the Norman Conquest and was first to be found in the area we now know as Lincolnshire and Yorkshire, and is originally from the Eure region of Normandy, famous today for Richard the Lionheart's ruined Chateau Gaillard and also Monet's house at Giverny. As so often, we have a divergence of opinion which is quite understandable when considering the translation of an almost extinct language and one which has certainly not left us its own Cornish to English dictionary or contemporary lexicon. Interesting too that St Ewe, near St Austell, is sometimes found as St Eva in old documents. Perhaps there is a link but it seems that the only consistent fact about the saint who gave their name to the parish is that she was female. Other details and accounts of her life vary depending on which source you look at. Again, as before, I am in no position to take sides on the matter, nor would I wish to. I simply offer the fact that nearly 70 per cent of the Eva families in England and Wales are in Cornwall in 1861, and others living elsewhere are Cornish by birth. There are none in Lincolnshire where some say the name originated, and just one Eva family in Yorkshire, headed by William Eva, a merchant mariner from Falmouth, Cornwall. Unless it has evolved into the much more common and universal name of Evans, I think I would be inclined to discount the Norman Conquest suggestion for the origin of the name and go with either of the Celtic origins.

It is a name spread right across Cornwall from Penzance in the west to Liskeard and beyond in the east. There is quite a concentration in and around the Camborne area where most, as would be expected for that area, are miners.

Property leases from the Arundell family archive still exist for lands leased to members of the Eva family in Crowan parish as far back as 1638, when both John and William Eva are described as 'Yeoman of this parish'. Included in the terms of a ninety-nine year lease to William Eva in 1694 are: 'one Capon yearly, one Harvest Journey and Heriot of one best Beast.' Terms and conditions of some of these old leases include items such as chicken, other farm fowl and animals, as well as a helping hand to the landlord at harvest time and the normal considerations of rent and keeping the place in generally good order. Even upon death of the tenant the landlord benefited; 'Heriot of one best beast' indicates that the landlord would receive the best cow or beef animal on the farm as his part of the deceased's estate.

FIDOCK

Again not a common name, but one believed to derive from *Budhek,* meaning 'victorious' in the same way as the name of Biddick, which is to be found earlier in this book. The name appears in various records spelt with either one 'd' or two, or as Fiddick. Variations in spelling are a part of any name study or family history search and are often attributable to the fact that until relatively modern time, most working folk had no real education and learning to read and write came a very poor second to earning a living.

Not all the Fidock clan have always earned an honest living though, as the case against William Fidock of Talland near Looe in 1774 demonstrates. He was found guilty of stealing goods worth just 1d from William Sawashman and his punishment was a public whipping. By the mid-nineteenth century though, most Fidocks are engaged in lawful employment and the small village of Newlyn East near Newquay seems to be something of a stronghold for the family name.

FOX

Here we have a name which is certainly not exclusively Cornish and which has no particular claim to derive from the Cornish language. However, I have included it because many of Cornwall's Fox families over almost three centuries have had such an influence on Cornwall and have contributed so much to the county, in so many ways, that they fully deserve inclusion.

The first prominent Fox family member to settle in Cornwall was Francis, who was related to the Earls of Ilchester in Somerset, and whose former home had been at Farley, near Salisbury in Wiltshire. He settled near St Germans and got married there in 1646 to Dorothy Kekewich of Catchfrench. Her family certainly had plenty of Cornish pedigree to share. Her maternal grandmother was Blanch Godolphin, from the family of Godolphin House, near Helston, whose Cornish associations date back at least as far as the Norman Conquest. Her maternal grandfather was a Killigrew, directly descended from Sir John Killigrew of Arwenack, whose Cornish connections track back at least as far as the mid-fifteenth century. So 'Cornish by marriage' as the slogan on my son-in-law's baseball cap proclaims!

Francis and Dorothy's second son, Edward, set up a business as a general merchant in Par near St Austell, later moving to Fowey. In 1762 Edward's grandson, George Croker Fox, established the family name in Falmouth, which was a thriving town and port, being much developed by the efforts of several notable and monied families. Among these were the aforementioned Killigrew family or 'the piratical Killigrews' as they had been known, who had turned their hand, shall we say, to many ventures during their several centuries of association with the area. Now, however, they were of the landed gentry class and Falmouth owes much of its early prosperity to them.

For George Croker Fox, prosperity came initially from his business interests as a shipping agent and ship owner and also as consulate official to many of the foreign nationals who came ashore in Falmouth. Among his many consulate duties was that of American Consul from 1794, the agreement documents being signed by George Washington himself. The Fox family were Quakers and much respected for their integrity and honour in business dealings. The hub of the Fox empire was in Arwenack Street, Falmouth, an imposing Georgian building with bow windows looking straight down onto Custom House Quay where much of Falmouth's and the Fox's trade came ashore. The building remained the Fox business headquarters for over 200 years, on the outside changing very little, but on the inside the business developed and evolved to suit changing times and markets, from the heyday of the Falmouth Packet service right down to the needs of the modern package holiday tourist.

Other family members were also making their mark in various parts of Cornwall. George's step-brother, Edward, settled in Wadebridge, and from that branch of the family emerged the Fox banking and textile manufacturing empire. Joseph Fox, George's younger brother, became a surgeon as did his three sons. One of these, another Joseph, was a joint founder and principal of the London Hospital. George Croker Fox extended his business interests to two of Cornwall's main exports of the time, pilchards and tin. Fox Stanton & Co. timber importers was also established at this same time in Plymouth and Falmouth, timber being much needed not only as a building material, but also to prop up the shafts and underground workings of the mines. That particular branch of the Fox business empire continued under this same name until it merged with a larger company as recently as 1957.

The Fox name became increasingly heard in the Cornish mining industry with the setting up of Fox's Perran Foundry in 1791. Their family home established near to this new business interest was at Tredrea, a large house overlooking the Kennal Valley where the foundry was built. The site had tidal access to the sea as well as a plentiful supply of fresh water coming down the valley to power a complex system of water-driven belts and machinery. From 1842 Robert Barclay Fox took over as manager and at its peak, Perran Foundry employed as many as 400 men, engaged in the design, casting and manufacture of all shapes and sizes of machinery and ironwork required by the mines. Steam power operated the mine machinery and Fox's Perran Foundry boilers became world famous and were cast in huge diameters, some large enough to literally drive a coach and horses through. As early as 1824, records exist of a shipment of 1,500 tons of mining equipment built at Perran Foundry across the vast Atlantic Ocean to Real de Monte in Mexico. When Cornwall's mines later began to decline as new mineral wealth was found in these far off places, many Perran Foundry machines originally set up in Cornwall's mining areas found a second life far away in places like Mexico, Peru, North America and Australia. They were carried across the oceans and reassembled in their new homeland by Cornish engineers such as Robert Harvey, himself a Perran Foundry man who went on contract to the Tocopilla Copper Mine on Chile's Pacific coast, accompanying a consignment of Perran Foundry mining equipment ordered by two Cornish exiles, Samuel Lean and John Jose, who had begun to develop the mineral wealth of that area.

Back in Cornwall, George Croker Fox junior, named after his father, married Lucy Barclay, a great grand daughter of the founder of Barclays Bank and his cousin, Robert Were Fox, married Lucy's sister, Maria. He became increasingly interested in science and was the first man to prove that temperature increased with depth underground. His mining interests brought him into contact with Richard Trevithick,

The semi-elliptical arch above the doorway at Perran Foundry, founded as Fox's Perran Foundry in 1791.

the Cornish pioneer of steam power, and it was Fox influence and money which helped Trevithick improve and develop steam power. Robert Were Fox began research into magnetism and a dipping magnetic needle made at Perran Foundry was used by James Clarke Ross to determine the magnetic South Pole. Fox himself was made a Fellow of the Royal Society in 1848 and two of his sons, Charles and Robert, were co-founders of the Cornwall Polytechnic Society in Falmouth in 1833. The society was granted Royal patronage in 1835 by King William IV and became the Royal Cornwall Polytechnic Society. The Polytechnic Hall in Church Street, Falmouth, was built in the same year and still houses the society to this day. Detail from the first annual report of the Cornwall Polytechnic Society, dated January 1833, gives an indication of Fox involvement and mention of other influential folk of the time. Sir Charles Lemon presided at the AGM. Lord de Dunstanville was Patron, with five Fellows of the Royal Society being Vice-Patrons. The original committee included, 'Dr Fox, Mr & Mrs R.W. Fox, Mr & Mrs G.C. Fox, Mr T.W. Fox, Mr G.P. Fox, Mr & Mrs A. Fox, Mr J. Fox, Mr & Mrs C. Fox of Perran, Miss Fox and Misses A.M. & C. Fox and Mr R.B. Fox of Bank.' Quite a family business!

As Lord Byron was once quoted as saying of Falmouth, 'The claret is good and the Quakers are plentiful.' The list of the family's achievements and their assistance to others goes on and on down each successive generation.

Money and influence also bought several large properties down the generations, including town houses in Grove Place and Woodlane in Falmouth and others on the outskirts, notably Penjerrick, Trebah and Glendurgan. At all of these, generations of the Fox family have created wonderful gardens with exotic plantings brought home by successive plant hunters from all corners of the world which can still be enjoyed today. Many Cornish folk throughout the past three centuries and more have reason to be grateful to the Fox family. Adopted Cornish perhaps, but worthy of note.

FREETHY

From *Freth* which means 'eager' or 'alert', this is a name with strong historical associations to the extreme south-eastern tip of Cornwall, around the parish of Antony, as far back as at least the fifteenth century. Here it is almost always spelt Freathy and there is a small village of the same spelling on the shoreline of Whitsand Bay.

Whilst researching this name I read a report about Freathy written by a coastal footpath walker which says, 'There is nothing else remotely like Freathy on the entire coast path. It is an entire community of holiday chalets, huts and shacks, seemingly in random layout.' The next part of the article saw the place as either 'a place of unique charm or an unsightly ramshackle mess.' Another account of the area from another coastal footpath journal tells of 'a very pleasant and mainly level walk along the coast road from Freathy to Tregantle Fort.' In the same way as I am happy to sit on the fence over the meaning of some names, I would offer both of these accounts and leave the rest to the reader. I have been to Freathy, I have cycled along the coast road there on the way to Rame Head and yes, there are a lot of chalets, but a mess? I would certainly say not. Most are extremely well kept and have some of the best views in Cornwall on a good day, overlooking as they do Whitsand Bay to the south and Rame Head to the east.

The Freathy families of this extreme south-eastern corner of Cornwall have the sea in their blood and many are listed with seagoing occupations. One such family is that of Edward Freathy and his wife, Hannah, formerly Hannah Boon from Brixham in South Devon. Edward was born in Wilcove near Torpont in 1813, son of Henry and Jane. He was baptised on 1 August 1813 in the Parish Church in Antony. Not surprisingly, being from an area almost surrounded by the sea and overlooking the Hamoaze and Devonport Dockyard, Edward went to sea at quite a young age. He worked on coastal vessels and this is how he seems to have met his bride, Hannah Boon, whilst she was employed in the household of Robert Farnaux, a ship builder in Brixham, helping to look after his eight children. They were married in Brixham in 1841, and soon afterwards Edward was posted to Ingoldmells in Lincolnshire in his new job as a coastguard. The coast here is a far cry from the rugged granite cliffs of his childhood in south east Cornwall. Soon he was moved to Lydd in Kent and helped to man the coastguard station there for many years. This was a much busier posting, being on the south-eastern corner of Kent where shipping turns north east to reach the busy ports around Dover and further on towards the Thames estuary. Edward remained a coastguard here for the rest of his working life and died in 1897 at the age of eighty-four. His widow, Hannah, lived on for another five years and died in 1902.

One of their sons, Alfred, born whilst they were living in Lincolnshire, also took to the sea and became a fisherman and lived for many years in a small cottage next to the Dungeness lighthouse. He also ran the British Sailor pub in Lydd for some years.

Edward and Hannah's second son, Henry also became a fisherman, as did their youngest son, George. Their eldest daughter, Hannah, married Robert Ditton, a Lydd fisherman, in 1877. One of the fishing boats he worked on was the *Thos Lezebeth*, a sixteen-ton lugger which was a regular visitor to Penzance on its long distance fishing trips. Sadly Robert died just a year after their marriage, leaving his widow with an infant daughter. They were a family whose close associations with the sea began in Cornwall and followed them through the next generation to the other side of England.

GEACH

—◦◦◦—

'Origin obscure' seems to sum up this name. Over two-thirds of Geach families in England in the mid-nineteenth century were either in Cornwall or of Cornish origin, so it has an obvious claim to be a Cornish name, but no one seems able to offer an explanation. Richard R. Blewett suggests that 'it is sometimes spelt Gaich, Gaych or Gaydge in Wills and Administrations and from 1569 to 1699, eighty are listed, so obviously a common name and one whose bearers had something to leave to the next generation, but its origin remains obscure.'

It is a name spread right across Cornwall but its main stronghold is in and around St Austell, where many are farmers. One Geach who was not a farmer was associated with the sea. He was Thomas Geach, born in Fowey in 1804, who became a coastguard. He moved to west Cornwall with his work and married Sarah Trenoweth Miller in Madron in 1826 and their first child, Lucinda, was born there. By 1841 they are living in Littlehampton in Sussex and have four children, Lucinda, Edwin, Cordeila and Sarah, the last three born in Sussex.

Thomas remained in Sussex for the rest of his life and later census records show him living with his two unmarried daughters, Lucinda and Sarah, in Littlehampton where he died in 1886. All three daughters became dressmakers but only Cordeila ever married. She married William Lock, a tailor in Littlehampton, in 1857 and the couple lived there for several years before moving to Portsmouth. Several family members of this generation and subsequent generations were employed in dressmaking and in the trade of tailor in and around Portsmouth.

GLASSON

—◦◦◦—

Derived from *Glesyn*, meaning 'green place' or 'grass plot'. Also offered variously as Glason, Glasan and Glassan, among other spellings, depending on the interpretation of the census enumerator or clergyman writing the entries in the parish register. Names are often subject to change in this way and nowhere is this more evident than when looking back to a time before universal free education. However you care to spell it, if you are a Glasson, you are, without too much doubt, of Cornish origin. The name has been around in Cornish records for several centuries, one of the oldest mentions being Thomas Glason, who was Reeve of the Manor of Roseworthy in 1584, on behalf of the Arundel family. A Reeve was responsible for overseeing the day to day running of the manor. This same Thomas Glason owned property in Penryn in the area known as Bohill.

GOYNE

—⁓—

The name of Goyne, sometimes offered as Goyen in older records, can not be found to have a Cornish origin in any reference work. About the only author who mentions the name is Richard R. Blewett in 1959 when he includes it in a 'non-Cornish origin' list. So why then are all but a handful of English bearers of the name here in mid-nineteenth century Cornwall? To be more precise, why are all but a small number of the bearers of the name to be found in one parish?

From my own research into parish registers and other material I can safely offer that if you have Goyne or Goyen in your ancestry, then your roots are almost certainly firmly in the shadow of St Agnes Beacon. My personal view is that its origins are probably linked to the Celtic word *Goon* which sometimes appears as *Gon, Gun, Goen* and *Woon* in Cornish place names and means 'downland' or 'open moorland'. The St Agnes region, with its high cliffs and the beacon area, typifies this aspect of Cornish landscape and so the name may have evolved here from 'men who lived on the downland'. The name of Goonvrea, meaning 'hilly downs' is to be found here in St Agnes as well as in many other locations in Cornwall. So why then did the name stick to this one small area? Like others we have seen already and will see later, there appears to be no logical reason for this, just a quirk of fate.

One St Agnes Goyne who made quite a name for himself was John Goyne. The 1841 census tells us that his widowed mother, Elizabeth, was running a boarding house at Polbrean, St Agnes, and that John had a younger sister, Mary, aged twelve, and two younger brothers, James, aged nine, and Francis, aged six. It is an interesting household at the time of this census with a variety of boarders, some of whom are miners but also

John and Margaret McColl, needle makers originally from Scotland, and James Washington, a sail maker born in 'foreign parts', as was his wife, Ann. There is also a shoemaker and a spinner living here, representing quite a mixture of trades, but all very valuable in an area where mining and the sea played very important roles in the life of the community.

John Goyne married Catherine Letcher in 1848. She was from another long established St Agnes mining family, who later branched out into business interests in the town, one of the family becoming a noted local watch and clock maker. By the time of the census of 1851, John and Catherine are living at British Row, St Agnes with two daughters, Louisa, aged two, and Emily, aged eleven months. John's occupation here is shown as tin miner, following on many generations of miners in the family before him.

Around 1854, John Goyne, by this time the father of four young children, waved his wife and family goodbye as he set out on the *SS Great Britain* for Australia. The *SS Great Britain* was the brainchild of that greatest of the great Victorian engineers, Isambard Kingdom Brunel. Oh to count him amongst the great folk who have come out of Cornwall!

By the year 1858 he was well established in the Bendigo area of Australia, where gold fever had struck. The discovery of gold here, as in other places around the world, brought tens of thousands in the eager hope of making a fortune. John Goyne had enough money to buy a plot of land at a place called Epsom. He built a small house there and opened a new business, the Stamper Grating Factory. The name says it all. Stampers were the crushing mechanism for the ore from which the gold was extracted, a process very much the same as the old Cornish Stamps which crushed the ore before the tin and copper were extracted. The grating was a wire mesh used to trap the gold particles after the stamping process was completed.

By inventing and developing a finer grating, John Goyne was able to produce a product which saved much more gold in the mesh than had ever been possible before, thus increasing the profitability of every single gold digging and stamping operation throughout the area. His invention became an overnight success and within a very short time, orders were being received for his new grating from all over the mining world. W.B. Kimberly in his *Bendigo and Vicinity* history of the area says, 'It would be difficult to estimate how much gold has been saved to the world by means of Mr Goyne's sieves.'

Back in England, John's wife and family anxiously waited for news of him with every ship which docked. The 1861 census shows them living at Rosemundy Hill, St Agnes. By this time the family is Catherine, aged thirty-one, shown as a gold miner's wife, with children, Louisa, twelve, Emily, eleven, Catherine, nine and John, seven. Finally in 1866 John felt that the time was right for his family to join him and he was reunited with them after an absence of over ten years. Catherine came first and helped plan a new house. The children followed about a year later and were soon settled into their new home, appropriately named *Rosemundy* after his own home area in St Agnes.

John and Catherine had three more children in Australia, of which one died as an infant. By the early 1880s, John Goyne had become a wealthy man. Shipments of English sheet iron and steel were arriving constantly at his factory to keep up with the production of his gold sieves. His property at Rosemundy had grown to an estate of some twenty acres, with the house, offices and factory all within its bounds. Six acres were turned over to orchards and the local newspaper of the time likened Rosemundy to 'a park, with trees, shrubs and gardens almost concealing the house.' A huge bay window faced on to the Bendigo Creek and a small stream meandered through the grounds.

Rosemundy was a large house, built of brick with large rooms, marble fireplaces, leaded window and unusual plaster features. It had a system of servants' bells and was later one of the first houses in Bendigo to be lit by electricity.

The factory often operated twenty-four hours a day to keep up with the demand for its product and on his retirement from the business, one of John Goyne's sons took over and the factory continued to make stamper gratings well into the 1920s.

They say that all the best ideas are quite simple and that necessity is the mother of invention, and here we have a simple piece of equipment, created and developed by one enterprising Cornishman who saw and met a need. With the profits of his labours, John Goyne was able to create his own little piece of paradise in what had been, just a generation before, a place where sheep roamed freely and people were a scarce commodity.

John Goyne died in 1907 at the age of eighty-one. A service was held at Rosemundy before the funeral cortege of the hearse, drawn by four draped horses and followed by four horse-drawn mourning carriages, left for the cemetery at White Hills.

John Goyne was a man who played no small part in the prosperity of the Bendigo mining area. To this day there is still a Goynes Road and Rosemundy Road in the area where he lived and Rosemundy, the house he named after his childhood home, still stands. It perhaps no longer echoes to the sounds of the servants bells, horses hooves and the factory next door, or even approached along a formal drive with impressive gates and picket fence, but it is there for all to see as a reminder of this Cornishman whose name is imbedded in the history of the area.

GRYLLS

This is a name with long associations with the Cornish legal profession. One part of the legal story began with the wonderfully named Samuel Theophilus Genn Downing who was a solicitor, commissioner for taking affidavits in all the courts, insurance agent for Sun Insurance, clerk to the local Board of Health and private resident of Trewergie, according to the 1873 *Kelly's Directory* of Redruth. The legal firm which bore his name had been set up back in 1836 in Redruth and, through several metamorphoses, has today become Grylls & Paige. But this is by no means the oldest reference to the name of Grylls being associated with the legal profession in Cornwall.

As far back as 6 September 1572, in the parish of Warleggan, a marriage is recorded between Charles Grylls Esq., barrister at law, and Agnes, daughter of Charles Tubbe Esq. of Lanreath. Charles came from a wealthy family in Tavistock, Devon. The couple had several children, among them John, later Sir John Grylls. He married into the wealthy Beere family and his grandson, again Charles, married into the Gerveys family of west Cornwall, whose ancestry around the parish of Zennor and later in Helston can be traced back to at least the fourteenth century. Add in a sprinkling of the Mohun family of Dorset along the way and you have quite a pedigree.

Reverend Richard Gerveys Grylls came from this line and that name is to be found no less than nine times as Mayor of Helston in the period 1794 to 1830, along with others of the same family, Humphry Millet Grylls, Thomas Grylls and Glynn Grylls, this last name confirming a Grylls association with the Glynn family of Glynn House, Bodmin. It is Glynn Grylls who is carrying on the family's 300 year association with the legal profession with the occupation of solicitor on the census of 1871 but before him his brother, the aforementioned Humphry Millett

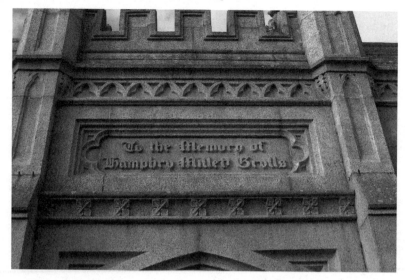

Above and right: Built in 1834 to honour Humphry Millet Grylls, this impressive gateway stands at the bottom of Coinage Hall Street, Helston, as a lasting memorial to this great man and other members of the Grylls family.

Grylls, banker and solicitor, had also made his lasting mark on the town of Helston. He was not only Mayor on several occasions but his actions also saved the nearby Wheal Vor tin mine and its 1,200 jobs. As a token of their appreciation the townsfolk erected a monument in his honour in 1834. This still stands proudly at the bottom of Coinage Hall Street. A copy of the Latin eulogy on a sheet of vellum written by Reverend Derwent Coleridge for the funeral of Humphry Millett Grylls was secured in a bottle and placed in a hole in the first stone to be laid at the south-western corner of the monument. It still lies there to this day.

But despite all the famous and not so famous folk associated with the name of Grylls, the origins of the name are somewhat obscure. There does not seem to be a convincing argument anywhere on its origin or meaning but, as with others in this book, over half of its bearers nationally are here in Cornwall in the mid-nineteenth century, making it a candidate for being considered Cornish.

It might seem strange to continue telling the story of members of the Grylls family by mentioning the name of John Couch Adams, noted Cornish-born scientist, discoverer of Neptune and a name we have seen before in connection with the Colenso name, but he was the son of Thomas and Tabitha Adams and Tabitha's maiden name was

Grylls. Adams was also much influenced by the teachings of his cousin, Reverend John Couch Grylls, who ran a school in Devonport where John Adams studied in his early years before going to Cambridge. Plenty has been written down the years on the work of John Couch Adams, but much less perhaps on his younger brother, William Grylls Adams. He was born, like John, in Laneast and the 1841 census shows him as the fifth of six children of Thomas and Tabitha still living at home. By this time John was away at his studies. William too showed much promise in his early education and, like John before him, went to university at Cambridge. He received his BA in 1859 and was appointed a lecturer in the Department of Natural Philosophy at King's College, London in 1863. He took over the post of Professor at King's in 1865 and remained for forty years. From 1878-80 he was President of the Physical Society and in 1880 he was elected President of the Mathematical and Physical section of the British Association for the Advancement of Science. He later became a Fellow of the Royal Society. Among his other diverse ventures he studied terrestrial magnetism, and also the relative benefits of oil or electricity as a means of providing the light for lighthouses. On the death of his brother John in 1892, William took those of his brother's scientific papers and manuscripts which had not been previously published and compiled them in two volumes, one in 1896 and the second in 1900. William died on 10 April 1915 at Broadstone in Dorset.

GUNDRY

From *Gun Dre,* meaning 'homestead on the downs', and the same as Goonvrea. This Cornish name has been spread as far as Shropshire and London in 1861 by its Cornish bearers. Richard Gundry, originally from Perranuthnoe is working in Shrewsbury as an engine driver whilst Mary Gundry, described as 'a lady' and originally from Goldsithney, is living by her own means in the St Pancras area of London. It is this western part of Cornwall around Penzance and up as far as the Crowan and Helston area which has the predominance of the Cornish Gundry families. Many are engaged in mining, as would be expected in these locations, and like so many of this era, the Gundry name can be found in the long lists of those who left these shores for a new life on the other side of the Atlantic Ocean. One such was John Gundry of Porkellis who set sail from Falmouth on Sunday 8 April 1849 aboard the *Roslin Castle* bound for Quebec, Canada, under the command of Captain Sadler. John, who was twenty-three years old at the time, wrote a very detailed diary of his journey which tells of everything from sighting porpoises, being becalmed on the Grand Banks, to the sad death of the baby daughter of William Williams, a mason from Constantine. His account also contains details of picking up survivors from the wreck of the *Maria of Limerick,* which had struck ice and sank. Of around 120 on board only a handful survived. John's journey was typical of thousands undertaken at this time when Cornwall's miners and many other tradesmen were being attracted by the promise of a better life in America and other far-off destinations. Places like Michigan, Wisconsin and other states heard the Cornish dialect for the first time. But John, like many others, was only about halfway to his final destination when his ship finally docked in Quebec on 24 May. He was bound for California, finally arriving there by a horse and wagon train in September 1849, after a six-month journey from Cornwall.

Back in Cornwall the Gundry family of Wendron can celebrate a famous son. Inglis Gundry was born in the Kingston area of London in 1905. He was descended from Cornish roots and very proud of it. His ancestors had gone to London to seek their fortune and made it, making shoes, but not just for anyone, a young Princess Victoria was among their customers almost a hundred years before Inglis was born. He always remembered his Cornishness and was Vice-President of the Cornish Music Guild and made a Bard of the Cornish Gorsedd in 1952, taking the Bardic name of *Ylewyth,* meaning 'musician'. He had already acquired a degree in Classics and Philosophy from Balliol College, Oxford and had a short career as a barrister before turning to music as a career in the mid-1930s. He served with the Royal Navy during the Second World War and afterwards returned to his musical career, being a regular contributor to the BBC Radio's *Music Programme* in the 1950s. Among his thirteen operas were two very much with Cornwall in mind. The first of these was entitled *The Tinners of Cornwall* in 1953 and another, *The Logan Rock,* was performed in the summer of 1956 at the open-air Minack Theatre at Porthcurno, within sight of the Logan Rock itself. Typical of Cornish summers, it rained on every performance after the opening night! So proud was he of his Cornishness that at the age of eighty he laid a commemorative wreath at the An Gof ceremony at Marble Arch in 1985. Inglis Gundry also edited many collections of Cornish hymns and songs from traditional folk music to Christmas carols. He died just short of his ninety-fifth birthday on 13 April 2000.

HAMMILL

Back in the year 1327, Roger Trehamel paid tax of 2s on a farm named Trehamel in Germoe parish. Today, the only remnant of that name is in Parc Trammel Cove, a small sand and shingle inlet about a mile north west of Porthleven on the Cornish coastal footpath. The location is a mile or so out from the fourteenth-century place name. Parc Trammel Cove sits today on the boundary of Breage and Porthleven parishes, with a boundary stone on the coastal path marking the fact. Germoe is inland a mile from the coast, but the name certainly appears to point to the same origin. The location is also one of several along this stretch of coastline where the returning Cornish Chough has been sighted in recent years. The name Trammel is associated with a type of fishing net, so what does this all have to do with Cornish surnames?

It is generally believed that *Hamil* or *Hamal* was a Celtic personal name and from this came *Trehamel,* the 'house or farm of Hamel' and that this later became the family name Hammill which we still find around Porthleven and Perranuthnoe in the mid-nineteenth century. Others have drifted away, but none of them too far from this home area of the name.

The name is also very much a part of Irish history and legend with mention of it amongst the Celtic peoples of southern Ireland as far back as the sixth century. So Celtic, probably, uniquely Cornish, probably not.

HAINE

Several spellings of this name have evolved down many generations including Hain, Haines, Hayn, Haynes and Heayn. It possibly derives from *Hen* meaning old but other sources suggest it is a personal name, possibly from the old Breton language where *Iahan* is equivalent to

Iohannes in the even older Latin form. We now know the same name as *John*. Another source suggests it is of Germanic origin in two parts, *Hech* meaning 'high' and *Narr* meaning 'fool' or 'jester', so a 'high ranking or King's jester'. Yet another explanation also gives Germanic origins but has a totally different meaning of 'dwellers in a hedged enclosure'. I am not so sure about these and prefer the Breton angle.

In Tregony parish is a place name going back to the fourteenth century which begins as Tregonhenyn and appears again as such a couple of centuries later; today it is Tregonhayne. This would mean 'house or farm of Hayne'. There is also Trehane not far away between Probus and Trispen which may also have similar origins. Whatever the original meaning, the name is spread right across Cornwall and well beyond in the middle of the nineteenth century and its common occurrence in other parts of England suggests either a non-Cornish origin, or more than one origin.

It seems that the Cornish version of Hayne is confined almost exclusively to the area around Camelford and Launceston, but if you add 's' to the end, you are more likely to be found further west around Bodmin or as far west as Truro. Hain is prominent around Redruth and St Ives whereas Hains is a mainly Bodmin interpretation. Obviously spelling was down to the census enumerator or churchman making the entries in the parish registers of baptism, marriage and burial in the early days, but these geographical differences also occur with other names and are reasonably consistent down several generations.

Mention the name of Hain in St Ives and you will doubtless be told the story of Sir Edward Hain. Born in 1851, he was of at least the fourth generation to bear the same name. The family business was shipping. At the time of Edward's birth the family owned just three small sailing vessels, trading mainly around the shores of Britain but in 1862 their ship *Emily* set off on a fifteen-month trip, taking in Canada and Brazil. Edward's first job was not in shipping but with Bolitho's Bank in Penzance, which we have come across before in this book. He later spent some time in London working with a tea merchant, and a combination of his banking experience and knowledge of foreign trade markets saw him quickly rise to prominence in the family company. So much so that in 1878 he issued something of an ultimatum to the company, of which his father was now in control, that either they modernised and bought new steamships, replacing, as he saw them, the out of date sailing ships, or he would resign. Financing this bold venture was a worry for his father, but the two came to something of a compromise agreement whereby one steamship would be purchased if Edward junior could persuade Bolitho's Bank and any other would-be investors to part with their money and back the project. The list of investors eventually included those from all walks of life, from the bankers down to local farmers, mine agents and even shopkeepers, all anxious to make a profit from this new project.

The first steamship ordered was named *Trewidden* after one of the Bolitho family homes in Penzance. She was built by Readheads Yard of South Shields who eventually built a staggering seventy-four ships for the Hain Shipping Company during Sir Edward's time in charge. Within a little over twenty years the company were running twenty-two steamships in full operation and the Hain Steamship Company Limited was formed. Edward had been elected a member of St Ives town council back in 1883 and was re-elected on five subsequent occasions. In 1900 he was elected unopposed as Member of Parliament for St Ives, taking over the seat from the retiring member, Thomas Bedford Bolitho. He held the seat until 1906 when he resigned to give his full attention to the shipping business. He remained prominent in local politics and social affairs and in 1912 was elected High Sheriff of Cornwall. By the outbreak of war in 1914, the company could boast as many as thirty-six ships with a further five on order. The First World War was to take a toll on the company and on the family. Two of its ships were trapped in German ports in 1914 and another in the Black Sea. During the war, about half of the 1913 fleet were lost to enemy action. Most tragic of all though was the loss of Sir Edward's only son, also Edward, in the Gallipoli Campaign on 11 November 1915 whilst serving as a Captain with the 1st Royal Devon Yeomanry. He lies buried far from home like so many of his generation, in the Hill Ten Cemetery near Aznak in Turkey.

The sad news shocked the family at their home at Treloyhan Manor on the outskirts of the town, and also the wider St Ives community. Sir Edward is said never to have fully recovered from the shock. He suffered a breakdown in June 1917 when in London during a German air raid, and although he returned to his home in St Ives, his health did not improve and he died three months later on 20 September 1917. He lies with others of the Hain family in Barnoon Cemetery, St Ives, on the hill overlooking the sea. Shortly after his death the Hain Shipping Company was sold to P&O, but its vessels remained an identifiable part of that company, as did the Hain practice of employing local St Ives men and boys and training them in the arts of seamanship. Many Master Mariners from St Ives have benefited from this practice down the years. The Second World War saw yet more Hain ships sunk by enemy action, the first of these being *Trevanion* which was sunk by the *Graf Spee* in the South Atlantic. Down the years the majority of the company's ships have borne Cornish names; *Trelyon, Tregenna, Treveal, Trevethoe, Tremeadow* and *Trevarrack* among as many as 101 bearing the Cornish name prefix *Tre-* that were registered between 1879 and 1922. These and others have proudly carried their Cornish names and crews all over the world.

HENDRA

From *Hen,* meaning 'old' and *Drea,* meaning 'farm', this name has been in Cornwall since the earliest days of family names. Richard R. Blewett, in his *West Briton* articles of 1959, says that the name has:

> Probably been around since the Saxon invasion of AD 460 when Celtic Britons were driven to the western fringes. Here they cleared lands and the population increased, new farms were established alongside those which had existed here before. In this way the two names of Hendra (old farm) and Trenoweth (new farm) would have come about.

One family on the 1861 census who neatly combine the two names is that of John Hendra (old farm) who is farming at Trenoweth (new farm) in Budock parish. John was originally from the Gwinear area of Cornwall where various census records show the name of Hendra mainly associated with mining.

There are many place names of Hendra in Cornwall. Part of Truro is known as Hendra, whilst there is also Hendra Downs near St Dennis, Hendra near Newquay and another near Stithians, to name but a few. The names of Hender, Henderson, Hendy and Hendry all appear to come from this common source and are all found right across Cornwall. Today the name of Hendra in Truro is associated with several businesses and going back as far as the nineteenth century the name is to be found connected to a wide variety of trades and businesses in the town. One particular nineteenth-century Hendra family line dates back at least as far as Thomas Hendra of Richmond Hill, Truro, who was a mason. He had a son, also Thomas, who became a coachbuilder. Thomas junior had three sons, one of whom, Richard, born in 1856, married Mary Jane Mills in 1879. She was the daughter of John Mills, a tailor originally from St Columb who had a business in Daniell Street, Truro. Richard was a plumber by trade with his business in High Cross, near the Cathedral.

Thomas was the second son, and he moved to Totnes in Devon where he married Sarah Jane Daw, the daughter of a bootmaker, in 1888 and followed his father's occupation of coachbuilder.

Henry was the youngest son, and he married Elizabeth Clemens, a draper's assistant. She was the daughter of James Clemens, builder of Castle Street, Truro. Henry later became a jeweller with premises in Pydar Street, Truro.

Whereas we often find three generations or more of one family all following the same trade or occupation, here we have one family, three generations and half a dozen or more different trades and businesses.

HOCKING

'Cornwall is the land of the Hockings.' So wrote one early twentieth-century researcher into the origins of English surnames. He was probably quite right, as about 75 per cent of England's Hockings or Hockens are here in Cornwall at that time and for at least a couple of centuries before. But the origins of the name? That is a different question. It may have links to *Hawkin* and *Hawken*, which itself may come from a line of seven Nordic Kings by the name of *Haakon*. It may be from a sixteenth-century personal name *Huchyn*. There is a Hocking River in Ohio, USA where the origins of the name are said to be from the Native American word *Hokhochen* or *Hokhokken*, meaning 'bottle shaped' and describing the shape of the river and its tributaries. It was known as the Hockhocking River until about 100 years ago when the name was shortened. So again, take your pick from a variety of sources, from Nordic kings to American Indians.

It is though a name which has made its mark here in Cornwall. The name of Silas Kitto Hocking may not immediately spring to mind when jotting down a list of famous authors, but he was the first author ever to sell a million copies of one of his books in his own lifetime. The book, *Her Benny*, tells the story of Liverpool street urchins and drew upon his own experiences of these children in Victorian Liverpool, where he was a Methodist Minister. It is a tale of survival in a very harsh environment, focusing on two main child characters who find Christian help in their fight against poverty and deprivation. It was Hocking's second novel and was translated into many languages. However, he himself made very little out of this book, as he sold the copyright for a mere £20. Very much more recently the story in the book has been revived as the basis for a successful musical stage play entitled *The Scouse Oliver Twist*.

Silas Kitto Hocking's background was far from what might be expected of a best-selling author. He was born in 1850, the son of James and Elizabeth Hocking, the Kitto middle name coming from his mother's maiden name. James was a miner who later became a mine agent and tenant farmer in St Stephen in Brannel on lands owned by the Boconnoc Estate. The children's names give some idea that religion played an important role in their upbringing. As well as Silas, named after a leading member of the Christian community who were followers of St Paul, there was also Tirzah, Mahalah, Simeon and Jabez from the Old Testament and Salome and Joseph from the New Testament.

Silas left Cornwall at quite a young age and is to be found in a variety of locations listed as a Methodist Minister in later life, including Newport, Monmouthshire, Burton on Trent, Manchester, Liverpool, Southport and Mansfield. On 29 September 1899 the local newspaper of the latter advertised that, 'To celebrate the twenty-first anniversary of the Mansfield Congregational Church, the Reverend Silas K. Hocking will conduct a service and will also deliver his popular lecture, "There's Nowt so queer as Folk". The Mayor of Mansfield will preside.' Was it then a Cornishman who 'invented' this old saying, usually associated with Yorkshire? I don't know but it is food for thought and, no doubt, disagreement.

In his later life Silas Hocking retired from his Methodist Ministry and became a full-time writer. He stood unsuccessfully for Parliament in Aylesbury in 1906 and Coventry in 1910 under the Liberal banner. A balding and heavily bearded man, he made a great impact during his lifetime, but sadly his contributions to Victorian and Edwardian English literature seem to have mainly been forgotten with his passing. One of his last works was an autobiography, *My Book of Memory,* published in 1923. He died in 1935 in Edmonton, North London at the age of eighty-five.

However Silas was not the only member of this Cornish farming family to find fame as a writer. Both his younger sister, Salome, and younger brother, Joseph, were also destined to become best-selling authors. Perhaps Salome's best known book is *Some old Cornish Folk, Characters from St Stephen in Brannel a century ago*. She moved away to Croydon in Surrey following the death of her parents and lived for a while with her younger brother, Joseph. In 1894 she married Arthur Charles Fifield, who was originally from Scotland and who had his own publishing business in Croydon, a convenient match for a budding author.

Joseph, the youngest of the family had also become a Methodist Minister. He studied at Manchester University and subsequently married Annie Brown in 1888 in Dewsbury, Yorkshire. She was originally from Newcastle, but the couple settled in Thornton Heath near Croydon, where the 1891 census shows Joseph as the Minister of the United Methodist Free Church.

Despite their similar backgrounds though, the books of the two brothers are often quite different. Silas' books generally have a moral message, his Methodist upbringing and preaching coming through. Joseph however wrote a much wider variety of books, drawing on his Methodist faith for some works but diversifying from commentaries and works relating to the First World War through to murder mysteries. His daughter Anne also became an author, her themes also including murder mysteries with such characters as Inspector Austen, Inspector Curtis and Sergeant Flyte normally solving the crimes.

HOLLOW

Generally thought to derive from *Hallow* meaning 'moorland', this name is found in many place names across Cornwall. Porthallow on the Lizard Peninsula, Penhallow near Newquay and at other locations. Hallew, between Bugle and Roche, is also of the same origin. As a family name though, it is almost totally confined to west Cornwall, with nine out of ten being found in the Penzance registration district, and the majority of those in St Ives and the adjoining parishes. A look at any nineteenth-century trade directory of St Ives will show many Hollow names in business in and around the town. For example, John

Hollow & Sons was listed as 'fish salesman, commission agent, coal, salt, paraffin, cutch, cork, net and general merchants, The Digey'. Another John Hollow was a coal dealer at The Wharf, Jane Hollow was a grocer of Fore Street and William Hollow was running the Golden Lion Inn, at Market Place in the heart of the oldest part of St Ives. William Hollow, mine agent is also to be found in nearby Lelant and several local farms are also run by Hollow family members.

The Hollow name today is spread far and wide. Some members of the family from the Redruth area were miners and their descendants are now to be found in America, Australia and New Zealand. Their ancestors were among the first to exploit the mineral wealth in these far off places when Cornwall's mining industry was failing in the nineteenth century.

One such was Joseph Hollow of Redruth. He was one of at least ten children born to Matthew Hollow, a Redruth mason and his wife, Mary. Joseph is listed on the census of 1841 as aged twenty with his own wife, Jane, living at Hicks Row, Redruth. His occupation is cabinet maker. He and Jane Thomas had married in Redruth early in 1840 when Jane was already expecting their first child. Sadly the child died at just a few weeks old in September 1840. There followed seven other children; Joseph, Fanny, Emily, Elizabeth, Charles, Alfred and Lucy. Of these Alfred also died as a child of around eight years. This family story so far is typical of thousands of this era with large families, the imminent arrival of the first child hastening the steps down the aisle and children dying at an early age because of poor diet, living conditions and medical facilities. In 1853 this 'journeyman cabinet maker', as he is described on the 1851 census, sought the better life being offered by emigration agents who toured towns and villages in Cornwall advertising free and assisted passages to a new life in far-off Australia. Joseph and several of his friends took this opportunity and sailed aboard the *Hibernia* from Liverpool in November 1853, bound for Melbourne, Australia. After a journey of three months, the ship finally reached its destination on 21 February 1854. His initial intention may have been to carry on his trade as a cabinet maker but gold rush fever took over his life and he travelled with his friends to Victoria. Here he worked initially at a place called Spring Creek. Over the next few years he stuck with mining, eventually becoming a shareholder in the McEvoy mine. Other Cornish names like Bawden, Dunstan, Oates and Davey are to be found associated with this mining area. By 1863 he was well established and sent for his family to join him.

They arrived in Melbourne aboard the *Red Rose* on 15 June 1864, having survived a potentially life threatening fire aboard the ship when off the Cape of Good Hope. On the passenger list are his wife, Jane with children Fanny, Emily, Elizabeth, Charles and Lucy. What happened to their other son, Joseph, named after his father, is unclear. It is thought that he may have joined his father in Australia before the rest of the family. Joseph senior appears to have remained in mining for the rest of his working life. He died in Australia in 1905.

HOSKIN

Perhaps you are a Hosken, Hosking, Hoskyns or even Hoskins, but they are all from the same *Heskyn,* meaning 'Sedge moor', according to most sources. There is one possible alternative and that comes from the name Osekyn. Robert Osekyn can be found in Poll Tax records of the county of Yorkshire as far back as 1379, with Peter Osekyn in Sussex around the same time. These names were said to have come from an old English word for 'a spear', but I can not find any corroborative evidence for this and so I will be happy to go with eminent Cornish scholars such as Robert Morton Nance, leading authority on the Cornish language and joint founder of the Old Cornwall Society, George Pawley White, former Grand Bard of the Cornish Gorsedd, and others when they give *Heskyn* as the origin.

The Hoskin name and its variants have strayed over the Tamar to a variety of places in England by the mid-nineteenth century, but from Millbrook to Morvah and Marhamchurch to Madron, the name can be found here in Cornwall in abundance. One intriguing bearer of the name was Cyril Henry Hoskins, born in 1910, the son of a plumber. He wrote a book entitled *The Third Eye* in 1956 in which he claimed to be the 'host' of the spirit of Tuesday Lobsang Rampa, a Tibetan monk and mystic. The book sold millions and the truth of the author's real identity was only revealed when it became the subject of investigation by private investigators hired by national newspapers. Hoskins, or Lobsang Rampa, also wrote a book entitled *Living with the Lama,* the text for which was apparently dictated to him by his Siamese cat, Mrs Fifi Greywhiskers. He was faced with ridicule and accusations of being a total fraud but said of these, 'I am Tuesday Lobsang Rampa; that is my only name, my legal name and I answer to no other.' He and his wife emigrated to Canada to get away from the scornful British public and media and he lived out his life there until his death in January 1961.

A rather more ordinary bearer of the Hoskin or Hosking name, and one for whose work I have a particular affection, was the late Eric Hosking. He was born in London in 1909 and became one of England's foremost wildlife photographers. I am not sure of a Cornish connection through previous generations of his family, but his work has been an inspiration to many over a long period of time.

Meanwhile back in Cornwall, another Hoskin of interest and intrigue was James Martin Hoskin. His Hoskin family had lived at Treassowe Manor in Ludgvan parish for several generations. Treassowe Manor is a very ancient place and was the seat of the Rogers family for many generations before they moved to Penrose, between Helston and Porthleven. They retained ownership of Treassowe and the Hoskin family became tenant farmers there. It is still to be found on modern maps of the area, about a mile north west of Ludgvan village on the road to Castle an Dinas.

James Martin Hoskin was baptised in Ludgvan Church on 8 March 1760 by the Reverend William Borlase, a family name to be found earlier in this book, and he married there on 3 June 1788. His wife, Elizabeth Vinnicombe, was a cousin to the St Aubyn family who boasted St Michael's Mount among their property assets. James was a great traveller; he wanted to find out how folk lived in other parts of England and even across the vast expanse of the Atlantic Ocean. Money was not a problem, the family were quite well off, and so James undertook his voyage to America at his own expense and wrote a book about it on his return with the rather lengthy title, *Narrative of a Voyage from England to the United States of North America with Travels through part of eight of the States and Remarks on the soil, produce, prices and agriculture in general.* He signed himself 'James Hoskin, Farmer' on the cover.

It seems, however, that James was not always an easygoing gentleman farmer, for he argued with the Reverend Stephens of Ludgvan and others concerning payment of tithes, an ancient system whereby the Church gained a percentage of income from property and land owners. So fierce was the argument that Reverend Stephens said that if he was still in Ludgvan when Hoskin died, that he would see to it that Hoskin was buried in the worst possible spot in the churchyard – the north side, often used in those days as a toilet area! Hoskin's answer to this was to buy himself a plot of land high on the nearby moors at Castle an Dinas. He had a wall built around this small plot of land and on his death in 1823, he was buried in this unconsecrated plot, as were two of his children when their time came. The story tells that his wife was also destined for this family plot but for unknown reasons, she and her late husband were not laid side by side in death.

There the story ended until 1964 when, because of the expansion of the nearby Castle an Dinas granite quarry, the remains of James, together with those of his son and daughter, were exhumed with all due dignity and Home Office consent. They were taken with their headstones by his Hoskin descendants for reburial at their present family home at Shillingham on the banks of the River Lynher, near Saltash, close to the ruins of the old family chapel. May he rest in peace there for eternity.

HUNKIN

If you are a Hunkin then there is an excellent chance that your roots lie in the south Cornish fishing village of Mevagissey. Either that or you are linked to one of a small handful of Hunkin families whose roots lie in Cornwall but who, by the middle of the ninetenth century, have gone across the sea as far as the Channel Islands, for there are at least four families in that category in the 1861 census. Add to that several who are Cornish but listed on board ships in various ports and harbours around the English coast and further afield, and you have not only a reasonable summary of the spread of the Hunkin name but also an occupational guide as well. The Hunkins were seafaring folk, some as fishermen and some as mariners aboard vessels of Her Majesty's merchant fleet.

One Hunkin of particular note sailed rather further than most. Matthew Hunkin was born in Mevagissey in 1815, the son of Matthew and Ann. Matthew senior was a shipwright by trade and his son also initially took to the sea for his living. He later joined the London Missionary Society, an organisation set up in 1795 who sent missionaries to Africa and the Pacific Islands. In 1834 the Society sent the first Western missionary to Samoa in the South Pacific. His name was John Williams. Williams travelled extensively over the vastness of the South Pacific island groups but one venture was to prove his last. Sadly he was killed and eaten by cannibals in 1839 whilst attempting to spread the Christian message to the islanders of Erromango, a tiny dot on the map in the Vanuatu Island group. Fortunately others, including Matthew Hunkin from Mevagissey, did not suffer a similar fate. Matthew Hunkin settled on Tutuila Island in the American Samoa island group and married a local girl, Fai'ivae Llaoa Aumavae, also known as Fatu Malala, in 1838. They had seven children, four sons and three daughters. He purchased land on the island and lived the life in keeping with the society which surrounded him in his new home. He died on 15 April 1888 and left his lands and possessions in his will to his wife and children. There then followed a very lengthy court battle over some of the parcels of land which the family claimed were theirs and which others claimed were not part of the original land sale, for which Matthew Hunkin had originally paid $100, 'or its equivalent in pork'... a wonderful way to pay your bills! The Supreme Court of Samoa finally decided on the case in 1906 and basically concluded that some of the land was legally Hunkin land and some was not.

A descendant of this same Hunkin line also features today in American politics. Eni Fa'aua'a Hunkin Faleomavaega junior, born in 1943, is the non-voting delegate to the United States House of Representatives from American Samoa.

JACKA

—◦◦◦—

Another distinctly Cornish name whose origins are obscure. I cannot find a reference source which is confident of the meaning of the name. It may be simply a Cornish form of the name James or it could have different origins, it is unclear. What is clear though is that it is a name which is associated with the highest honour for military valour. Albert Jacka, son of Nathaniel, whose family were migrants from St Buryan in Cornwall to the mining areas of Victoria in Australia, was born in 1893. Like so many he joined the army in 1914, serving first of all as a private with the Australian Imperial Force. He later found himself part of the Anzac forces at the Battle of Gallipoli in 1915 and here, on 19 May, the Turkish forces launched an attack on the Anzac trenches. During this attack Albert Jacka, together with three others, attacked a section of the Turkish-held positions, Jacka himself being the only one to survive the attack. He personally shot five Turks and bayoneted two others before the attackers fled. He held the position single-handedly for the rest of the night and the following morning his platoon commander, Lieutenant Crabbe, found him alive and alone amongst the bodies of the Turks and his allied comrades. Crabbe said that he would recommend Jacka for an honour for his action and his bravery, and on 23 July 1915, the following citation appeared in the *London Gazette:*

> His Majesty the King has been graciously pleased to award the Victoria Cross to the under-mentioned Officers and Non-Commissioned Officers:
>
> No 465 Lance Corporal Albert Jacka, 14th Battalion, Australian Imperial Forces.
>
> For most conspicuous bravery on the night of 19th–20th May 1915 at Courtney's Post, Gallipoli Peninsula.

Albert Jacka was the first Australian recipient of the VC in the First World War. His bravery did not end there and many other acts are recorded against his name, each sufficient to merit recognition of his brave conduct. He received rapid promotion to Captain after his VC incident and his picture was used in all manner of recruiting posters and other material supporting the war effort back home in Australia and further afield. After the war, he returned home where he gave many years of faithful service to his home town of St Kilda. Here, he and a couple of his former army colleagues started an electrical goods import and export business, but he is perhaps remembered most for his contribution to civic life in the community. He was elected to the St Kilda council and became Mayor in 1930. Sadly his life was to be cut short. He collapsed after a council meeting in December 1931 and died on 17 January 1932, just a week after his thirty-ninth birthday. His pallbearers to St Kilda cemetery were eight other VC recipients and an estimated 6,000 people lined the funeral route. His VC is proudly displayed at the Australian War Memorial in Canberra and an annual service is still held in his honour in his home town of St Kilda, such is the respect and fond memory of this Australian citizen of Cornish pedigree.

JELBERT

—⁓—

If you are a Jelbert, or even a Jelbard or Jilbert or one of several other spelling interpretations down the past 400 years or so since Johannes Jelbarte was baptised in the parish of Gulval on the outskirts of Penzance, then your roots are firmly in that part of Cornwall. This is another name which is mainly confined to one small area. The parishes of Madron, Gulval, St Just and St Buryan are home to over 70 per cent of the total English population of the name. Its origins are again obscure. Not for the first time do we have a name from this small corner of Cornwall whose origins are unclear. Do they speak a different language down west?

The Last Will and Testament of the late Johannes Jelbarte or John Gelbert, named above, certainly gives a few spellings we would find odd today but generally it is not a foreign language! It is reproduced here in part, transcribed verbatim from the original held at Cornwall Record Office. He begins:

> The 17th daye of October 1664. In the name of God Amen. I John Gelbert of the parish of Madderne in the Countye of Cornwall being sicke in bodye but of perfect minde and memorie praise be given to god doe make this my last will and testament in manner and forme following. Inprimis I give and bequeth my soule into the hands of my blessed maker and redeemer and my bodye to be buried in the parish Church of Gullvall

He goes on to leave 5s to his son, John, 3s to his grandson and 2s to his daughter Welmett. His son Peter will receive £5 when he reaches twenty-one and for his wife he bequeaths:

> My desire is that my wife live with my sonne James as longe as she liveth and to have as often as need requires the use of a horse to ride with such things as maye be nessesarye for her use and if it happen that she be disposed to live elsewhere that James my Sonne paye her six pounds a yeare & as after the desease of my wife to leave it to him againe as also one fielde of Land In Polmearewartha of the parrish of Zennor to her disposinge called or named parke an Crigoe.

His son, James, also receives his late father's interest in lands at Trithall in Gulval parish, along with land at Vellin Noye and a part share of a stamping mill and other property in Madron parish.

John was an important man in the local area. He had also served as a churchwarden in his time. Subsequent generations of this family have been farmers and seafarers. John Gilbart, grandson of the above John Gelbert, served aboard HMS *Discovery* and HMS *Cumberland* in the early years of the eighteenth century. He died at sea in 1707 off the coast of Jamaica. He left his whole estate to his widow, Elizabeth, which included lands at Pednventon in Madron parish. This is next to Boswarva, a farm held by his brother, William. Both are situated on the uplands to the north of Madron village, on the road leading across the Penwith Moors to the north coast. It was not a very productive farming area, being exposed to all winds and weathers and with only a thin covering of soil over the granite beneath.

The family remained in this part of west Cornwall for several generations, farming at locations in Gulval, Madron and St Hilary parishes. William Gelbard, six generations after the original John, was a farmer at Tregurtha in St Hilary parish and when he died in 1838, he left his estate to his widow, Jane, and the 1841 census shows her there with her children Jeremiah, William and Patience.

The name of Jeremiah Jelbert and others can be found in census and other records well into the twentieth century, in and around the parishes of Madron and St Hilary and all can trace their ancestry back through ten or more generations in this part of Cornwall. Even today, the name is still associated with agriculture in this area of Cornwall overlooking St Michael's Mount and Mounts Bay.

JOSE

'Contrary to popular belief this is not a name which comes from Spain, it appears in St Ives Subsidy Rolls in 1523, some sixty-five years before the Armada.' So says Richard R. Blewett in his *West Briton* article on the name in 1959. Others suggest it is a Romano-Celtic name from the Latin *Joseus*. So it is certainly a name which has been around for a very long time and one with three-quarters of its bearers in 1861 living in Cornwall.

It is spread from St Levan in the far south west all the way to St Gennys and St Juliot in the north east. But there is a very big gap in the middle of the county where there are none. This batch of half a dozen Jose families in the far north east of Cornwall is over fifty miles from their nearest Jose cousins in Truro and further west. Again, either an anomaly of the evolution of the name, or one Jose moving east in the 1700s leading to a small collection of them a couple of generations later – who knows?

But the north-eastern and the more western and southern Jose families have one thing in common; most are farmers. There is the odd tradesman thrown in for good measure and also the odd miner in one or two areas, but it is a name mainly associated with agriculture.

One Jose family member though, who was to make his name neither in farming or mining, was Richard Jose. Born on 5 June 1862 he was the eldest of six children born to Richard and Elizabeth Jose of Lanner. The 1871 census shows the family living at Lanner Green. As with all mining families of the time, life was harsh and dealt some bitter blows. The youngest child of the family died young and soon afterwards in 1876, Richard senior died at the young age of just forty. This led to a dramatic decision in the life of young Richard Jose. He sailed to America, alone it seems, at the age of around fourteen or fifteen in search of an uncle who had gone there some years before to work in the mines of Nevada. He never found his uncle, but what he did find was an entirely new career away from mining which was to make him a household name across America. He had a talent for singing and sang to the Cornish miners of Nevada in the bars to earn a crust and subsidise his earnings from a job as a blacksmith with another Cornish exile, William Luke. The 'Singing Blacksmith', as he became known, caught the attention of everyone with his counter-tenor singing. Among his admirers was Alfred Doten, a journalist from Virginia City who kept a detailed journal of life in these mining towns from 1849 to 1903. These were later published and one early encounter with Richard Jose reads:

> Dicky Jose, a young man of about nineteen years old and resident of Reno …having one of the finest tenor voices I ever heard. He favoured us with several popular ballads with others to accompany him. He was later over at the Hole in the Wall saloon and there he sang and bands played.

Richard Jose's popularity as a singer grew and within a few years he was commanding a wage of $100 a week, many times more than he would have earned had he stuck to being a miner or a blacksmith. He travelled America from San Francisco to New York, playing to full houses. In the 1890s he toured Europe on several occasions, singing for various heads of state. On a tour of South Africa's mining areas, where he would have encountered many fellow Cornishmen, it is said that Cecil Rhodes closed down his diamond mines for a day so that his employees could listen to Jose in concert. An organist at one concert in Montreal, Canada, stopped playing when Jose was singing, so awestruck was he by his voice. The early years of the twentieth century saw great expansion in the invention of film and sound recording techniques and Richard Jose signed up with one of the early recording companies, The Victor Talking Machine Company, for whom he recorded what was to become his best known song, 'Silver Threads among the Gold'. In 1915 a silent movie of the same name appeared, with Jose singing in the wings and filling Madison Square Gardens with his voice as the silent image of him flashed before the captivated audience.

Soon afterwards his singing career ended. There are two versions of the reason for this. The first is that early radio, with its narrow bandwidth and low fidelity, did not give a very good reproduction of his singing voice, so his popularity faded. The second is that he was hit on the head by a falling stage curtain with such force that not only were stitches required, but his hair turned from black to white overnight and his voice was also affected. Whatever the reason, this stocky Cornishman with a magnificent and powerful voice lived out his days in San Francisco, where he died on 20 October 1941 at the age of seventy-nine. American friends of Richard Jose later presented a trophy in his honour to be contested each year by Cornish choirs.

Here the story may have ended with the voice and the name of Richard Jose fading away into the mists of time, but recent discoveries of some old recordings of his music in America and modern techniques have allowed a re-recording of his voice in a modern format by two stalwarts of all things Cornish, Chris Blount and Joe Pengelly. It is well worth a listen.

JULIAN

—₪₪—

'Another borrowing from the Romano-Celtic' according to several reliable sources. This name has been around as a place name since at least the early fifteenth century, when Nanshelen appears in St Just in Penwith parish, evolving through the sixteenth-century spellings of Nanselyn and Nangelyan to become Nanjulian by 1748. This name is still to be found at the end of a narrow road which runs beside Land's End Airport and out almost to the cliff edge, about as far west as it is possible to get on the Cornish mainland. It is a place of ancient relics, cairns and tumuli from pre-Christian times and mine workings scratched out of the cliffs. These are often a copper-green colour from centuries of leaching of the ore from deep inside their rocky faces and in more modern times, deeper mine workings, many even out under the sea. Names like Geevor, Levant, Wheal Owles and Botallack are to be found hereabouts and conjure up all the magnificence, harshness and tragedy of Cornish mining. It is easy to believe then that the Romans came here to trade with the early Celtic Cornish for copper and tin and left behind a relic of their civilisation in the names of the folk who lived here.

Half of the Julian families in England are in Cornwall in the middle of the nineteenth century, with others born here and living away from their native county. Examples are Thomas Julian who has taken his family and his knowledge as a mining agent to Wales, and also the sisters, Sarah and Eliza Julian from Cornwall who are seeking their fortune working in London as servant girls in a large house.

One of the classic photographs of old Truro, taken around 1890, shows the bottom of Lemon Street with 'John Julian & Com'py' on the large signboard above the ground floor and another board on the wall advertising the business as 'Auctioneers & Valuers'.

An advertisement from 1873 shows the business as 'Jno. N. Julian, Builder, Surveyor, Cabinet Maker', and also adds upholsterer, undertaker, house agent, appraiser, valuer for probate, house decorator and paper hanger to the list. As if that were not enough to keep one family happy, they also offer roofing and other felts, they are agents for the North British and Mercantile Fire and Life Insurance Office as well as offering 'funerals furnished with economy and despatch.'

A 1910 advertisement for the business shows them as auctioneers, valuers, house agents, general house furnishers, undertakers and furniture removers, with 'new large dry Repositories specially built, branches at Newquay and Falmouth.'

It is a name which was part of Truro's commercial history for well over 150 years. John Nankivell Julian appeared on the scene with his baptism on 9 December 1817, son of John and Nancy. The Nankivell came from his mother's maiden name and his father was a gardener, originally from the village of Probus, who had come to the fast growing town of Truro to work.

John N. Julian appears with his parents and working as a carpenter on the 1841 census and the family are living at Fairmantle Street in Truro. By 1861 he is living with his wife, Ann, five daughters, three sons, father, step-mother, cousin and two servants, all in the same house in Fairmantle Street. Now shown as a builder, he probably needed his skills to add an extension to the house for all these occupants!

By 1871 he is on the census as a builder and upholsterer, employing twenty men and six boys. John Nankivell Julian died at the age of just fifty-eight in 1876 and the business was taken over by his son, John junior, who moved into the premises at the bottom of Lemon Street. He had married Sophia Gostling, daughter of a Norfolk boot and shoe manufacturer in Norwich in 1880. How he came to be in Norwich to meet her is something of a mystery, but after the marriage they returned to Truro where they continued to evolve the business to match changing times. John Julian & Son remained a part of Cornwall's house moving and furnishing business scene for many more years after the passing of the original owners.

KEAST

There are two very different interpretations of the origins of this name. One is that it is from the personal name *Kest* and can be found back as far as 1350 in the place name *Lankest* in St Ive, meaning 'enclosure' or 'land of Kest' (a personal name). This name has evolved into *Keason* in more recent times. The second is that it is from the same word *Kest*, which is a 'straw basket' in the old Celtic tongue, so it would mean a name for 'folk who make straw baskets'. As with other names in this book, this name occurs in other parts of England by the mid-nineteenth century but has four out of every five of its bearers here in Cornwall or of Cornish descent and so 'qualifies' as Cornish for our purposes.

Its spread is quite general, but with larger concentrations in and around Truro and the Liskeard area. There is a suggestion that the poet John Keats should really be John Keast and that his father, Thomas, was a Cornishman who went to London to seek his fortune, and there married and remained for the rest of his days. I can find no real supporting evidence for this theory but it is a possibility which several sources mention.

KELLOW

Derived from *Kel* meaning 'shelter' or *Celli* meaning 'grove of trees', both have the *ow* suffix which is an accepted way to make a name plural. Again a difference of opinion on derivation but as we have said before, there is no definitive lexicon or dictionary written down by our ancestral Celtic cousins so we rely on scholarly interpretation and judgment and on occasions this varies.

Place names such as Kellow near Looe have evolved from spellings of Kylyou and Kelyou as far back as the fourteenth century. Kelly Bray in north Cornwall translates as 'grove of trees on a hill'. The first written record of the Killiow estate near Truro, which derives from the same source, dates back to the year 1170. A sixteenth-century play in Cornish, *Beunans Ke*, features a healing spring at Killiow, said to cure leprosy. The spring is still in existence, perhaps not needed much these days for lepers but a pleasant addition to the new life of the park as a golf course. The Killiow family lived at the estate from as far back as the thirteenth century, so the name as a family name has been around at least as long and it was passed down through many generations until 1785. It was then bought by Robert Gwatkin, whose wealth came mainly from his grandfather's packet ship and mining businesses. His wife was a cousin to Sir Joshua Reynolds. Financial losses forced him to sell and the estate was purchased in 1814 by the Daubuz family, wealthy mine owners and tin smelters from Truro. William Daubuz was High Sheriff of Cornwall in 1850 but the family were forced to sell up because of changing times in Cornwall's mines and a loss of the family fortune. Killiow lay almost unnoticed and untouched for decades, briefly featuring as a billet for troops in the Second World War. Since then it has been given a great deal of tender loving care and improvement and a new lease of life as a golf course alongside the working farm.

As a family name, Kellow is found across Cornwall but predominantly in the middle and east of the county, from St Austell through to Liskeard, Bodmin and the Camelford area. Here it is slate quarrying and not deep mining which is the major industry and Kellow families are to be found in St Teath and Delabole working in the slate quarries. One such family was that of William and Charity Kellow. Both were born in Tintagel. William was the son of Moses and Jenny Kellow of Trewarmet. This generation and previous generations of the Kellow family were slate quarry workers. Charity was the daughter of John and Maria White, a farming family originally from north Devon. William and Charity married in 1860 and their first son, named Moses after his grandfather, was born in 1862. Soon after his birth the family moved from Cornwall to Ynyscynhaiarn, near Pothmadog in North Wales, another area well known for its slate quarries. William became manager of the Tan y Bryn quarry in Lanfrothen and young Moses also worked there as a commercial clerk. In 1895 the Croesor slate quarry near Penrhyndeudreath in Merionethshire was reopened under the managership of Moses Kellow, who by now had an excellent all-round knowledge of the industry and had become a successful slate quarrying engineer and manager. Having been closed as unprofitable back in 1878, Moses Kellow built up the Croesor quarry and its neighbour the Parc quarry under one company, producing as much as 5,000 tons of slate a year. Unlike most Cornish slate works, which are open cast, these two quarries were totally underground. Kellow was the first man to use electric locomotives in the quarries and also patented a new type of hydraulic rock drill, which increased productivity and efficiency. Both quarries prospered for many years but both finally closed by 1930. Moses Kellow died in 1943 at the age of eighty-one.

KESTLE

It may be that your version of this name is Kessell or Kestell or even another variation, but without doubt it is derived from *Kestel* meaning 'an earthwork' or 'castle'. It is a place name in many locations in Cornwall. There is Kestle Mill near Newquay, the village of Kestle between Mevagissey and St Ewe, Kestle Farm, Ladock and Kestle on Frenchman's Creek on the Helford estuary to name but a few, all of which can be found with a quick look at a map of the county. Long-held associations with fortifications and earthworks probably makes this a very old name indeed, for as long as man has had farm stock or families to protect from wild animals or other human predators, he has built walls around his land. Whether it is a simple hedge, wall or wooden stockade or a much grander fortification or castle, the basic idea is the same - to keep things from getting out or to keep things from getting in. It is not the most common name, far from it, but that does not detract from its right to a place here in our book.

One Kessell family with at least ten generations of Cornishness behind them now run a car sales and garage business with several branches in Cornwall, whilst the much loved and fondly remembered Edgar Kessell MBE was the founder of both the Treverva and Holman Climax Male Voice Choirs, as well as Mabe Ladies Choir and did so much for choral singing in Cornwall for over forty years until his retirement in the late 1970s. A memorial cup in his name is still the top honour to be won by male or ladies choirs at the Cornwall Music Festival.

One Kestell who has a small town named after him is Reverend J.D. Kestell. He was a South African chaplain and fought alongside General de Wet during the Boer War and was also one of the peace negotiators with the British in 1902. The small township of Kestell in Eastern Free State, South Africa, was founded in 1905, just south east of the site of the Second Boer War Battle of Groenkop when General de Wet defeated the British. Kestell died in 1941 and had the honour to be buried alongside General de Wet and President Steyn at the National Women's Monument in South Africa. This monument stands as a lasting tribute to the suffering of women and children during the Boer War. Also buried there is another Cornish person, whose name and brave deeds are probably far better known in South Africa than they are here in her home county. She was Emily Hobhouse, born the sixth of eight children to the Reverend Reginald Hobhouse of Liskeard in 1860. When she heard of the awful plight of women and children suffering at the hands of the British in concentration camps in South Africa, she campaigned tirelessly for their welfare. She later went to Russia to help some of the poor and oppressed caught up in the 1917 Revolution there. When she died in 1926 her ashes were taken to South Africa at the specific request of those who remembered her work.

KEVERNE

St Keverne on the Lizard Peninsula is the obvious home of this name. The name appears at least as far back as the *Domesday Book* of 1086, which says, 'The Canons of St Achebran's hold eleven acres of land for ploughs, twenty acres of pasture with eight cattle and thirty sheep.' The original Cornish name for the village seems to have been Lannaghevran. The saint after whom the village is named is shown as Achebran in very early records, which down the years became Akeveran by 1200, then Keveran by 1340 and Keveron by 1596. However, scholars such as Dr Borlase have argued over whether Kiaran or Keyran is the correct name for the saint who gave his name to this place, and there has even been argument down the centuries that Kiaran is one and the same as Piran, our Patron Saint of Tinners who, so legend would have us believe, famously floated across from Ireland on his millstone, around AD 460. Whatever the true historical origins of the name it is sufficient to say that it is a very ancient name associated with this particular corner of Cornwall.

In the mid-nineteenth century there are several Keverne families in St Keverne, all of them farmers, and the name has not spread very far despite being an ancient one. Those who have ventured as far as Camborne or Truro have places of birth on the Lizard Peninsula such as St Martin in Meneage, Cury and Ruan Minor, so it is a name whose origins are very much confined to this one small part of Cornwall. Going back twenty years to the census of 1841, the confinement of the name to the Lizard area is even more pronounced.

Michael Joseph, or An Gof, as he was popularly known, was born in St Keverne and he it was, together with Thomas Flamank of Bodmin, who led the 1497 Cornish Rebellion to London. Sadly it ended with their motley army dispersed and the both of them being hanged, drawn and quartered, but it is still the stuff of legend and remembrance among Cornish folk everywhere.

One of the oldest surviving records of the Keverne name in St Keverne comes from the Subsidy Rolls of 1524, where the name of Thomas Keveryn is to be found. The Arundell Archive, a huge collection of documents relating to this once extremely important and influential Cornish family also gives reference to 'Helwyn in Sent Keveryn' as far back as the early sixteenth century, so the name has been in the area for many hundreds of years.

KITTO

—◦◦◦—

Sometimes with 'w' added to the end, this name is generally accepted to mean 'Christopher's children'. Religious connections to the name of Christopher are many centuries old. Legend relating to a man of this name carrying the infant Christ across a swollen river led eventually to his beatification and Saint Christopher became the patron saint of travellers. The name appears in ancient Greek stories as Christophoros, which translates as 'bearer of the chosen one'. Consider then why a name with associations dating back probably a couple of millennia and more, and with a worldwide Christian following, should find itself confined as a family name almost entirely to one small corner of England.

Perhaps the Celtic tongue has, not for the first time, given us a name whose origins are, in fact, lost in the mists of Bodmin Moor. Our acceptance of the scholarly derivation from the Christian name of Christopher is similar to our acceptance of the derivation of several other names we have seen already where 'origin is obscure', or where the name appears to be centuries old but confined to a very small area. My personal, and perhaps non-scholarly view, is that somewhere down the centuries we have simply lost some of the old language and its meanings and that as a result, some derivations are 'best guess' rather than verified fact. That is not to say that a good deal of scholarly work has not gone into the search for a meaning, but simply, as I have said before, we do not have a comprehensive and contemporary lexicon or dictionary left over from Celtic times.

But what of the bearers of the name itself? There are only about 300 Kitto names to be found in England on the 1861 census with about 250 of these living in Cornwall or of Cornish origin. Of the Kittow spelling, there are less in overall numbers but an equally high proportion in Cornwall.

The name is, yet again, one where a single parish dominates. This time it is the turn of the area between Helston and Penzance, and Breage parish in particular, to have a majority of the Kitto families.

One such in 1861 was the family of John Kitto, described as a retired miner, with his wife, Margaret, and two sons, John, thirty-seven and Joseph, twenty-three, both described on the census as 'gold miner, late California'. Both had been to California in the gold rush era and had returned to their native county, perhaps richer, perhaps wiser.

Other Cornish Kitto families from this same area are to be found in census and other records in many of the great mining areas of the world. Some arrived in America and became early iron ore mining pioneers in places like Marquette on the Upper Peninsula of Michigan.

Others arrived in the 1850s at Port Adelaide and spread to the gold mining areas in southern Australia. One of these was Richard Luke Kitto from Gwennap. He is to be found in Bendigo in 1857 where he is working as a mine manager and using his skills, influence and education to help develop the infrastructure of the area. He later became a member of the Legislative Council of Victoria, but is perhaps best remembered for his work in setting up funds in the thriving gold mining areas in Australia, subscribed to by the miners themselves, many of whom were of Cornish extraction, to help alleviate the poverty and hardship being felt at the time back in some of Cornwall's mining areas. Kitto returned to Cornwall and personally made the necessary arrangements for hundreds more out of work Cornish miners to emigrate to Australia, providing much of the funding for their passage and for their initial accommodation from his own resources.

Another man with the same name of Richard Kitto was a boat builder in Porthleven, and the family name has been associated with that trade there for at least three generations. Boats from their yards found their way to many of England's principal fishing ports. The first mention of his name though is not directly associated with the building of boats, but in a dramatic sea rescue. In 1847 the King of Norway sent a letter of congratulation to Richard Kitto of Porthleven for his part in the rescue of crew from the Norwegian schooner *Elizabeth*, which had been wrecked off Porthleven in 1846. Kitto had initially been an apprentice with Symons boat yard of Penzance but within a few years he had started his own business. As well as building fishing boats for Cornish fishermen, Kitto's company also made the nets to catch the fish, bringing the first net making loom to Cornwall in 1853. By the end of the nineteenth century, Kitto & Co. were employing as many as a hundred men in their yards. Kitto-built fishing boats were to be found in most of the UK's principal fishing ports, such as Lowestoft, Yarmouth and Aberdeen, as well as across the channel in many French ports.

Small coastal trading vessels were also built and orders even came from as far away as the Hudson Bay Company in Canada for two motorised vessels, specially designed to survive the ice of Arctic waters. The first of these was the *Fort Churchill,* completed in 1913. She sailed the Atlantic bound for her new owners, only to be firmly gripped by the Arctic winter in September of 1913. A massive piece of the ice broke away later in the year and floated off, taking the *Fort Churchill* with it. That it seemed was the end of the vessel and an order was made for a replacement, named the *Fort York.* However, nearly a year and about 800 miles away on the coast of Greenland in August 1914, the *Fort Churchill* was found, fully intact and serviceable. This was a cause of great pride among the men of Kitto's yard whose tiny vessel had proved more than a match for the Arctic ice packs.

Even when fishing vessels were in much less demand in the austere years between the wars, the Kitto factory remained in business, making nets for fishermen and also diversifying into making nets for use across a much wider market spectrum, which included customers in the horticultural industry and even the goal nets at Highbury Stadium for Arsenal Football Club.

KNEEBONE

Ernest Weekley was professor of Modern Languages at Nottingham University from 1898 to 1938 and wrote extensively on etymology, the study of the source and development of words. However, the Cornish family name of Kneebone seems to have stumped him. Weekley said of the name 'the least said about it the better' and he admitted that he had no idea where it had come from and could not interpret its meaning.

For Mr Weekley and others, the name has nothing at all to do with bony parts of the leg, its origin is in the Cornish place name of Carnebwen, which from the fourteenth century down to the modern day has evolved though 'Carnebon' to become the place name still to be found in the parish of Wendron in Carnebone, Carnebone Farm and Higher Carnebone, straddling the A394 Falmouth to Helston road.

Carnebwen translates as 'Ebwen's rock pile', so it is a place where a man called Ebwen dwelt, somewhere in Wendron parish, where the high ground is littered with rocky outcrops.

Wendron, Helston and Stithians have their fair share of the name and many of those who have strayed as far as Launceston and Liskeard in the east of Cornwall have their roots in these more western parishes.

The Kneebone name, like so many, has however been carried worldwide by some of its bearers. Joseph Kneebone married Mary Martin Reed, another family name with centuries of association with the Wendron area, in 1860 but a few years later he left his wife and four children behind and went off to the gold mining area of Nevada County, California. He sent for his family in the early 1870s and they settled into a farming community. One of their sons, Andrew Reed Kneebone, became one of the best and most respected teamsters in the area. Teamsters were an essential part of any mining or other industrial operation in the nineteenth century, as they were the heavy goods vehicles of their day, hauling loads with their teams of horses. The name has stuck down to the modern era in America where the drivers of huge modern road transport are also known as teamsters.

Other Cornish Kneebone families are to be found in records of mining areas around the world. One such is the family of Henry and Elizabeth Ann Kneebone. They left the ailing Cornish mining industry behind and are to be found in the Australian mining area of Wallaroo, where their son Henry was born in March 1876. Henry Kneebone was educated in Kadina and at the age of twelve began working as a copper miner. His mining career was short-lived and after just a year, he joined a local newspaper, the *Kadina and Wallaroo Times*. The tempting prospect of making a fortune in the Murchison goldfields in Western Australia took him there in 1894 but, like most gold prospectors, he found nothing to make himself rich and by 1899 he was back in the newspaper industry with the *Coolgardie Miner*. He married in 1903 and gained promotion to managing editor of the *Coolgardie Miner* by 1906. He was a founding member of the Typographical Society of Australia and also a member of the Western Australia Workers' Association. He returned east in 1910 and joined the *Daily Herald* in Adelaide. Between 1912 and 1916 he worked in London for the Australian government as press officer at the High Commission. On his return to Australia he took up the cause of the Labour Party and by 1922 he was Party President. Henry Kneebone continued campaigning work with the Australian Labour Party right up to his death just before Christmas 1933.

LAITY

—〜〜—

A name derived from *Leth* meaning 'milk' and *Chy,* meaning 'home or house'. So Laity families were probably originally dairy farmers many centuries ago. By the middle of the nineteenth century, many were still farming but many others spread themselves between those other two traditional Cornish occupations of mining and fishing. Porthleven and the surrounding parish of Sithney, where we have just met the Kitto name, have its fair share of Cornwall's Laity families as fishermen and mariners. The Laity families a little further west around St Hilary are mainly farmers whilst the Laity families of inland parishes around Redruth provide miners. Again it is a name confined to a small area with very few east of Helston. Those living away from Cornwall also show strong links to this western part of the county.

The place name of Laity also appears several times around Cornwall.

LANDER

—〜〜—

From *Lan Tyr,* meaning 'enclosed church land' or 'glebe land', although an alternative of *Lan Dar,* from 'oak enclosure', is also a possibility. Despite its probable Celtic origins, the name of Lander is found in many locations from Cornwall, through the West Country to Gloucestershire and well beyond, as far as Yorkshire in the north and Cambridgeshire in the east. So is it as Cornish as its suggested origins would have us believe? Again, it is a matter for debate and discussion.

Cornish Lander families are, unlike some names in this book, spread far and wide across the county from Penzance in the west to St Germans in the south east and Camelford in the north east. The most famous of Cornwall's Lander families was undoubtedly that of Richard and John Lander. They were born in Truro at the Fighting Cocks Inn, which was situated on the quayside of the then busy port with ships and crews from all corners of the known world coming and going all the time. Little wonder then that Richard acquired a taste for adventure and exploration and left his schooling at a very early age. He walked to London at the age of nine looking for adventure and two years later, at the age of eleven, set off for the West Indies in a merchant ship, with, it seems, little or no money or possessions, simply a desire to see some of the places he had obviously heard about in his father's inn as a small child.

When still only nineteen in 1823, he made his first exploration trip to Africa, visiting the Cape of Good Hope. In 1825 he accompanied the Scottish born explorer Lieutenant Hugh Clapperton on a trip to the River Niger, to map the area and explore its potential wealth on behalf of the fast expanding British Empire. Clapperton died in Africa and Lander returned and published the expedition's findings in 1830. Later the same year he went again to the area, this time in the company of his brother John. They journeyed hundreds of miles inland by canoe looking for the source of the Niger. Richard Lander was awarded the first gold medal of the Royal Geographical Society upon publication of the account of this journey in 1832. His next expedition to this same area was to be his last. He was killed by natives at Fernando Po in 1834. His name lives on in Africa as well as in Cornwall. In Africa you will find Truro Island and Cornwall Mountain, named by Lander, and here in his native county you will find the name of Richard Lander associated, among other things, with a school in Truro and the man himself atop a column overlooking his home town.

This fine statue was sculpted by another Cornishman, Nevill Northey Burnard. Among his other commissions were Richard Trevithick, the steam engine pioneer, and John Wesley, the Methodist preacher. Sadly Burnard died a pauper in Redruth Workhouse despite his undoubted talents. That we have the Lander Monument at all is purely an accident, or should that be a series of accidents. If Lander had returned alive and triumphant, the Truro town council had decided to honour him with a medal or silver salver to mark his achievement, but when news of his death was received, plans were necessarily changed and the decision was taken to erect a monument in his honour instead. The first attempt ended in disaster when the column fell down, and the second was much delayed and not completed until 1852, nearly twenty years after his death, by which time his brother and fellow explorer John had also died. It appears that bureaucracy ground slowly even in the nineteenth century.

Above: The inscription on the Lander Monument tells of the tragic early death of Richard Lander.

Left: Truro's monument to its most famous son, Richard Lander.

LANYON

Lanyon Quoit is perhaps one of the most iconic of Cornwall's ancient monuments. It stands beside the road from Morvah to Madron and has attracted casual visitors, students of our ancient history and photographers of all abilities for centuries. Its huge granite form dates from an era well before Christianity and although it may not be as grand as it was before it fell down in a violent storm in 1815, it is still as mysterious and mythical as any of the names we have looked at so far. The Lanyon name comes from *Lyn Yeyn,* meaning 'cold pool' in the Celtic tongue, and is found in various place names across Cornwall. Another possible source is given by William Bottrell, whose story appears on page 42 of this book, in *Hearthside Stories of West Cornwall*, which tells the story of 'Nancy Trenoweth, the Fair Daughter of the Miller of Alsia'. Nancy we shall meet again on page 176, but in setting the scene for the story, Bottrell says:

> About two centuries ago an old farmer of the name of Hugh Lanyon, with his wife and only son, resided on a lonely farm of Bosean, which is situated on the brow of the hill overlooking the vale of Penberth…Old Hugh Lanyon, according to the family tradition was descended from one of the two brothers who came to this part of the world, from the town of Lanion in Bretagne, about the time of Edward II.

So again we have two possible origins of the name but when you consider that Bretagne, the area we now know as Brittany, and Cornwall share a common Celtic origin, probably both are of the same meaning.

As a family name its Cornishness is in no doubt with over 90 per cent of its bearers either in Cornwall or of direct Cornish descent in the 1861 census. Go back twenty years to the 1841 census and the Cornishness of the name is even more pronounced. Although the spread of the name is wider than some we have seen, there is little doubt that the Lanyon heartland is, like Lanyon Quoit, firmly set on the moors of West Penwith. The place name here of Lanyon has come down from at least as early as the thirteenth century as Linein, Lenein and Liyayn before arriving at its modern spelling. Farmer, miner, shoemaker, tea dealer and even currier are Lanyon occupations in 1861, a number of them running their own small businesses in Penzance. The Lanyon name has found prominence in a variety of circles around the world. Colonel Sir William Owen Lanyon was a prominent Victorian army officer and British Administrator in South Africa, whilst Sir Charles Lanyon was a noted architect, also of the Victorian era, who is responsible for many of Belfast's finest buildings, from churches through to the Crumlin Road gaol and courthouse. He also surveyed many roads in the province, was Mayor of Belfast in 1862, MP for the city from 1865 to 1868 and held many other offices and business interests, from harbour commissioner through director of a flax making company to Grand Master of the Irish Freemasons. Quite a respectable list of achievements for the son of a Royal Navy purser with family links to Cornwall.

One other Lanyon before we move on was Peter Lanyon. Born in St Ives in 1918 he had a career in the RAF during the Second World War and thereafter returned to his first love of painting. His artistic abilities earned him work and commissions in several countries, including Italy and America to name but two. However, his true home was always in his home town of St Ives where the surrounding coast and countryside was the inspiration for much of his work.

MADDERN

To quote directly from *Lyson's Topographical and Historical account of the County of Cornwall, 1814:*

> Maddern, Madron or Maddron, in the Deanery and in the west division of the Hundred of Penwith, lies about a mile and a half nearly north west from Penzance, which is a Chapelry of this parish and is the Post Office town. The principal village in the parish is Lanyon.

Not only does this give us the location, but also the origin of this family name and a direct link back to the name of Lanyon which we have just met.

Yet again we have a name whose origins go back many centuries but whose spread is very confined. All but a very small number of

Madderns in Cornwall live in the Penzance district and all but a handful of them live almost within earshot of the eight bells of St Maddern's Church, Madron.

Madron is recorded in the *Domesday Book* as being under the jurisdiction of the Manor of Alverton and the parish itself covered the whole of the area now within the much newer parish of Penzance.

MAGOR

Derived from the Celtic for a wall, particularly an old or ruined wall, this name is quite widespread across Cornwall and as we look at this name, it seems a good time to make a cup of tea.

Richard Manuel Blamey Magor was born in Truro in 1844, the son of Martin Magor, and his wife, Elizabeth, formerly Manuel (or Mannell as it is more commonly spelt). Martin and Elizabeth were married in the late 1830s. The Magor family were drapers in Truro. Richard's father, Martin, had followed his own father, also Martin Magor, into that line of business and they had premises in St Nicholas Street. However, Richard was destined to carve a career very far removed from the drapery business.

He began work as a commercial clerk but in 1865 he set sail for India, where he became assistant manager of the Great Eastern Hotel, Calcutta. Just four years later, in 1869, he joined with James Hey Williamson to form Williamson Magor, a tea growing and exporting business. Tea had been known in Britain since the middle of the sixteenth century and had become very popular amongst those who could afford it. The price of tea at the time was such that it was still a drink of the upper classes. At that time, tea imported into Britain came from China and the British, through the East India Company, had established trading posts in China for tea as far back as 1684. The Chinese supply became more and more unreliable for a variety of reasons and new areas were sought where tea could be commercially grown. One of these was Assam, taken over by the British in 1826. Native growing tea was found there a few years later and within a generation this once mainly jungle area was destined almost to become one giant tea plantation. George Williamson, brother to James Hey Williamson and known as 'the father of India's tea industry', set up plantations and the necessary factories and other infrastructure to process and export the tea to an ever growing tea drinking British market. 1858 saw the transfer of India formally from the East India Company to the British Empire and with this came even more British investment in India and its tea industry. By the time Magor and Williamson got together, success was almost guaranteed as the market seemed to have an insatiable thirst for tea.

Good business practice and mergers with other companies soon made Williamson Magor a hugely successful company. It was run by managers for the family owners who were in the habit of visiting for a few months each year, in theory to oversee the running of the business but in practice it was as much to get away from the British winter weather. Into the twentieth century expansion continued both in India and in Kenya, a relatively new tea growing area, which was also at the time governed as part of the British Empire. The company is still run today by direct descendants of the same Cornish Magor family, providing quality teas to a worldwide market.

MANHIRE

All over Cornwall, particularly on some of our unspoilt moorland areas, you will see ancient stone circles, field systems, burial chambers, standing stones and a host of other reminders that this land has been occupied and farmed over several millennia by people about whom we know very little apart from the small clues they have left behind in these historical sites. In more modern times we have named them, and names such as The Blind Fiddler, Two Sisters, Boswens and Gun Rith all relate to one type of ancient relic, the 'Menhyr', or standing stone.

Often 10ft or more tall, these stones are things of mystery and legend. Some say that names like Blind Fiddler and Two Sisters are reminders of those who stand there now for eternity, having been punished and turned to stone for dancing or playing on Holy Days. Whatever their original purpose, and that has been the subject of centuries of research, guesswork and speculation, the word 'Menhyr' has passed down the centuries as a family name. Manhire, Minear, Mennear and several other variations are all named after these relics of a bygone age.

'The Blind Fiddler', a Manhyr, standing about 10ft tall in a field just off the main A30 west of Penzance. Such relics of the pre-Christian era are scattered right across Cornwall.

MANNELL

—ᴍᴍ—

Here again we have a difference of scholarly opinion on the origin and meaning of this name. Three possibilities emerge about equal for the true meaning. The first is that it is simply a Cornish form of the name Emmanuel. The second is that it derives from *Maen,* meaning 'stone' and *Huel* or *Whel,* meaning 'workings', giving us 'stone workers/workings' or 'quarrymen'. The third is that it derives from *Maen,* meaning 'stone' and *Howel,* meaning 'vigilance', so 'stone of vigilance' or 'lookout post'. Any of the three seem quite acceptable and again I am not taking sides, just giving options based on my own findings. There are also spelling variations, the most common of which is Manuel, which we have mentioned above under the Magor name.

There is a Manuels Farm near Newquay whose name has evolved from Maenhulwois in the thirteenth century to Maynuwals about a hundred years later, and eventually to the modern spelling. This confirms that the name has been around for a long time, but either the second or third option could be made to phonetically fit these early spellings and so as it does not exactly give any vital clues to origin, we will move swiftly on.

Most nineteenth-century Cornish Mannell families live in the middle part of the county and many are miners. Looking at various census and other records, it is apparent that many also spent time in other mining areas around the world. Joel Mannuel from Truro married Martha Buckingham in 1854 and the couple spent some time in the silver mining area around Real de Monte in Mexico before coming back to Cornwall. There are other Cornish Mannell families who stayed in their new countries and have descendants spread far and wide across the mining regions of North America, from California to Michigan and Pennsylvania. Mannells born around Grampound and Probus are buried in Australia and yet more are to be found in South Africa's diamond mining areas.

NANCARROW

This name means 'valley of the stag', with *Nans* being 'valley' and *Carow* being 'stag' or 'deer'. This is the generally accepted derivation of this very Cornish name. A name which has spread across Cornwall down the years, its main centre is in the Redruth area where some, as might be expected for that area, are miners but others have a variety of trades and occupations.

The name of Nancarrow is closely associated with the former Phoenix Rope Works in Illogan where rope was made for many of the mines of the area. Further east, the name of Nancarrow is associated with the trade of tanning in Grampound where the family, along with the Croggan family, made Grampound a centre of excellence in the tanning and leather working trades. William Nancarrow of Grampound later took his skills further east and set up a tanning works at Burraton Coombe on the outskirts of Saltash. He was at least the third generation of his family to be employed in the tanning business. His father and brother, both named Thomas Nancarrow, were engaged in the business in Grampound for many years. The previous generation of the Grampound Nancarrow family was headed by Walter, also a tanner by trade.

One sad note on the Nancarrow name relates to William Henry Nancarrow, son of Robert Nancarrow, a mine engine driver from St Austell, and his wife Elizabeth. William Henry married Mary Cannon in St Austell in 1897 and they had eight children. Like his father before him, William Henry became an engine driver. He secured employment with a company in Yonkers, New York State, through his uncle, Mr Alexander Robins, who was born in St Austell but who had been in America working for some years. Mr & Mrs Robins, came back home to St Austell to visit family and friends late in 1911 and returned home to America taking their nephew William Henry Nancarrow with them, to work alongside Mr Robins. The rest of the Nancarrow family were due to join him at a later date. The fateful journey to New York was booked as a third class passenger on the *Titanic*. Like so many others, William Henry Nancarrow was lost when this great ship foundered on her maiden voyage across the Atlantic Ocean. His body may have been recovered but was never formally identified. The bodies of his aunt and uncle were recovered by the *MacKay Bennett* and positively identified from personal belongings found on them. Their bodies and their recovered possessions were returned to their grieving daughter in Yonkers for burial.

The *Cornish Guardian* newspaper of 26 April 1912 records these sad events as follows:

It is now almost certain that Mr W.H. Nancarrow and Mr Alex Robins have gone down with the ill fated liner. Hopes were held that at least Mrs Robins might have secured a place in the rescue boats, but now that the *Carpathia* has reached the shore it is all too probable that she too went down with her husband. Though Mr & Mrs Robins have been absent from this country for a number of years, a very large circle of friends greeted them on their arrival in the district last autumn... When he decided on the date on which he would return to his country of adoption, and found that it was necessary to travel on the *Titanic*, it was said that he was somewhat troubled in his mind, having an objection to going on a maiden voyage.

Mr W.H. Nancarrow was the son of the late Mr Thomas Nancarrow, of Buckler, and followed the occupation of engine driver. He was well known in the district as a singer of some ability and frequently made the rounds of the neighbourhood with carollers at Christmas time. He was going out to seek his fortune in company of his uncle, Mr Robins. With his wife and family of eight children, much practical sympathy has been felt and it is probable that at some of the chapels in the locality, offertories will be taken on their behalf.

The Reverend J.T. Morris, preaching at the Methodist Church, made reference to the *Titanic* disaster and expressed sympathy with the bereaved of the district. The hymn played as the ill-fated ship was sinking was sung by the congregation.

William Henry Nancarrow is not the only Cornishman we have met who perished in the freezing Atlantic waters on that terrible night in April 1912. One other we have met already was Cornish born Stephen Curnow Jenkin of St Ives, see page 67. But they were not the only Cornish folk aboard the *Titanic*. As many as sixty-four men, women and children from Cornwall were aboard and few survived. Among those who perished was William Carbines, also from St Ives. He was on his way to join his two brothers who were mining in Michigan, but instead they were later to return to St Ives with his body, laying it to rest with other family members in Barnoon cemetery, the only Cornish victim known to have been brought back home for burial. Among the survivors of the tragedy was the helmsman at the time the ship hit an iceberg. He was Newlyn born Robert Hichens. Although criticised by one or two passengers, the subsequent enquiry found that he had no chance of taking evasive action quick enough to avoid the tragedy. However, the episode blighted his life and he suffered severe stress for many years. In 1933 'whilst the balance of his mind was disturbed', as reports suggest, he pulled a gun on a man in a dispute over a boat in Torquay. In sentencing him to five years in prison the judge said he had passed a lenient sentence because of his ordeal aboard the *Titanic*.

NANCE

From *Nans,* meaning 'valley' as we have seen with Nancarrow. So it means 'dwellers in the valley' as opposed to Bray, 'dwellers on the hill'. It is a name which is certainly of Celtic origin but, like many we have seen, is certainly not among the top ten by sheer weight of numbers in the county. However, when it comes to compiling any list of anything Cornish, the name of Nance can not be passed by or ignored, and it is probably one of the reasons why books such as this are written today.

It was Robert Morton Nance, born in Wales of a father from Padstow and a mother from St Ives, who did so much to revive an ailing Cornish culture and identity. Robert Morton Nance spent his early years in Wales before moving to St Ives in 1906. This was his ancestral home, with a long history of seafaring in the family. He developed a love, indeed a passion, for all things Cornish, his particular interest being in the revival of the ancient Cornish Celtic language. In 1920, together with another scholar of the Cornish heritage, Henry Jenner, he formed the first Old Cornwall Society in St Ives. Jenner was already many years into his quest for knowledge of the ancient peoples of Cornwall, their language and customs, much of which was studied during his time working at the British Museum in London. The joining together of these two like minded enthusiasts and researchers was the reason for an immense revival in Cornish culture, language and customs in the 1920s and 1930s.

Left: The simple slate headstone of Robert Morton Nance in Zennor Churchyard. He founded the first Old Cornwall Society and was joint founder of the Cornish Gorseth.

Below: Zennor Church, mentioned under the names of Nance and Quick.

Within three or four years of the formation of the first Old Cornwall Society, there were societies in many towns right across Cornwall. Nance published his *Cornish for All* in 1929, which represented many years of work studying the old language, its origins and meaning from scant scraps of material left from an almost forgotten era. He and Jenner formed the Cornish Gorseth together in 1928, with Jenner elected as its first Grand Bard. Nance became the second Grand Bard on Jenner's death in 1934. Robert Morton Nance continued to research and spread the Cornish revivalist message for the rest of his life. In his lifetime, Cornwall's people again recognised their Celtic roots. The Cornish flag was now to be seen flying proudly and Cornishness was being promoted politically. He died in 1959 at the age of eighty-six and is buried in the churchyard at Zennor.

The inscription on his headstone reads, *Oberow y vewnans yu y wyr govath,* 'his life's works are his true memorial'.

Perhaps somewhat overshadowed by his younger brother Robert, the name of Ernest Morton Nance is one which may not be as familiar here in Cornwall as it is in his native Wales. Ernest was born in 1868 and graduated from Oxford University to a career teaching classics at Swansea Grammar School. He began a collection of Welsh porcelain and pottery and in addition to being an avid collector, also made a comprehensive study of Welsh porcelain, the factories, manufacturing processes and all things associated with his subject. His book, *The Pottery and Porcelain of Swansea and Nantgawr*, was first published in 1942 following a lifetime of study and collating data and detail. He spent his final years in the family's home town of St Ives and upon his death, his collection of around 1,500 items of Welsh pottery and porcelain was donated to the National Museum of Wales.

NINNIS

This name has the same origin as Enys and means 'well watered land'. It is a place name in over a dozen places across Cornwall, and as a family name it is as close as you will come to being exclusively found in Cornwall.

To narrow it down a little more, in 1861, our datum point, about two-thirds of the Ninnis families in Cornwall are to be found in the west of the county, and looking even closer, most of these are fishermen from St Ives. Again then we have a name which is certainly many centuries old, but in all that time has spread only a short distance. Again, I can offer no real explanation for this when other equally ancient names are spread far and wide.

In looking for many of the Cornish folk who have borne some of the family names we have looked at in this book we have travelled to many countries of the world, but for a short biography of one member of the Ninnis family we must travel even further than we have done already.

The story begins in St Austell at Christmas 1798 with the baptism of Paul, son of Paul and Joanna Ninnis. Paul junior left Cornwall in his teenage years and, like so many, went to London to seek his fortune. Here he met Julia Pratt and the couple were married in St Paul's Church, Covent Garden, in June 1828. St Paul's is also known as 'the actor's church' because of its location and long association with the theatrical community in that part of London. The couple had several children, among them Belgrave Ninnis, born in 1838. He obtained medical qualifications and practiced for a while at St Thomas' Hospital, London, before, like so many Cornish Ninnis names before him, chose a career at sea and rose to become Inspector Surgeon General of the Royal Navy.

He also had a taste for adventure and because of this and his medical qualifications, he was chosen by the British explorer Captain Sir George Strong Nares for his Arctic expedition of 1875-76. Belgrave Ninnis married Ada Jane Sutton in 1883 and in the late 1880s, travelled with his employment from England to Hong Kong before returning to live in London early in 1891. Their eldest son, Belgrave Edward Sutton Ninnis, was born in January 1887. He joined the army and became a Lieutenant in the Royal Fusiliers. He too had a keen sense of adventure, inherited from his father, and in 1911 he joined the Antarctic expedition led by the Australian explorer, Sir Douglas Mawson, a veteran of polar exploration, having been to Antarctica in 1907 with Ernest Shakleton and again a couple of years later with Edgeworth David. Mawson had turned down a chance to go with Scott's group on his ill-fated race to the South Pole, preferring to prepare for a more science-orientated expedition of his own, funded in the main by the Australian Association for the Advancement of Science.

Belgrave Edward Sutton Ninnis joined Mawson's expedition as a handler for the dog teams. On 10 November 1912, Mawson, Ninnis and Xavier Mertz, a Swiss explorer who had also represented his country at the Winter Olympic Games, left their base camp to survey King George V Land. Just over a month and 350 miles from base camp on 14 December 1912, whilst crossing a glacier, Ninnis fell through a snow-covered crevasse, together with the team's main sledge, six dogs, most of their rations, their only tent and other essential equipment. He was never seen again and his body never recovered. Mertz and Mawson immediately turned and made for base camp but with few fit dogs and the most meagre of food and shelter, their progress averaged just a few miles each day. The extremes of weather and shortage of proper food and shelter meant that they had to eat meat from their remaining dogs. This caused Mertz to become ill and on 8 January 1913, still 150 miles from base camp and safety, he died.

Mawson carried on at a snail's pace before he finally reached safety in early February. Ninnis Glacier was named by Mawson in honour of his lost colleague. Certainly to my knowledge, it is the remotest memorial to a man of Cornish descent anywhere on the planet. Mertz Glacier, in that same remote and desolate part of the globe, is named in honour of his colleague who also perished.

The Ninnis dynasty also produced yet another polar explorer, Aubrey Howard Ninnis, a cousin to Belgrave Edward Ninnis, who was an engineer on Shakleton's 1914-16 Ross Sea Party in the Antarctic.

ODGERS

The origins of this name can be found as far back as Viking times in the seventh century as *Hrod-Gierr*, meaning 'famous spear'. From here it spreads to some of the Germanic tribes as Odger or Roger and seems to have come across the English Channel in pre-Norman times. Earliest surviving references in Cornwall appear in the parish registers of Helston, St Keverne and Mullion in the early years of the seventeenth century.

It is generally agreed that it has no root in the original Celtic tongue, but despite its ancient associations with Vikings and Germanic tribes, three out of every four in the country live in Cornwall or have Cornish associations in the mid-nineteenth century, and so it is included as a Cornish name. The name is spread across the county from Penzance to the Devon border with a concentration around the mining areas of Gwennap and the farms of Stithians. But to follow an Odgers biography, however, we again travel many thousands of miles to the other side of the world.

William Odgers was born in Falmouth in 1834, of a family closely associated with the sea. He followed the family tradition and joined the Royal Navy in 1852. By 1854 he was in the Baltic helping to prevent Russian ships from leaving to take part in the Crimean War and by the late 1850s he was on the other side of the world, where he saw action in the China Wars, or Opium Wars as they have become known. On the ship HMS *Niger*, he soon found himself in New Plymouth, New Zealand. This was also a time of war in this part of the world with the British fighting the native Maori tribesmen. In March 1860, at the height of the Taranaki Maori War, a contingent of British troops was sent to rescue settlers in Omata who were considered vulnerable to Maori attack. The whole episode descended into something of a muddle when the regular troops accompanying the party turned back, their orders being to return to New Plymouth before nightfall. The rest of the volunteer militia engaged some Maori fighters and the shots were heard back in New Plymouth, upon which a naval detachment was sent to help out. Among those in the crew was William Odgers. As soon as they arrived at the scene of the skirmish they were ordered to retire by the senior British officer, Lieutenant Colonel G.F. Murray, who said that he had the situation under control. However it seems his orders were either not heard or simply ignored and, possibly spurred on by the offer of a £10 reward by a senior officer, a small raiding party led by William Odgers captured the Maori flags which flew above their stronghold. Their actions created such confusion amongst the Maori defenders that the army contingent was able to re-group and return to New Plymouth without fear of further attack. Odgers and the Navy men returned by sea to a heroes' welcome. Despite ignoring the orders of the senior officer present, Captain Peter Cracroft, who led the naval raiding party, was commended by the Admiralty. Lieutenant William Blake, who was wounded in the action but who continued to fight, was promoted to the rank of Commander and went on to have a distinguished naval career right up to his death in 1874 off the coast of Africa.

William Odgers was awarded the Victoria Cross, the highest and most prestigious award for gallantry in the face of the enemy. He was also offered promotion, which he declined. *The London Gazette* of

3 August 1860 reads, 'On 28 March 1860, William Odgers displayed conspicuous gallantry at the Storming of a Pah during operations against Rebel Natives in New Zealand, having been the first to enter under heavy fire, and having assisted in hauling down the enemy's colours.' A 'Pah' was the name given to a Maori defensive enclosure.

Not wishing to dampen the bravery of this Cornishman, later reports suggested that his actions were perhaps not as heroic as reports of the day put forward. They vary considerably and many are no doubt embellished by a good old tot of Navy rum. There is even one suggestion that by the time Odgers and his band reached the fortification that it was 'defended' by just one old woman, who was killed by the attackers. The other, more warlike, defenders were at the time heavily engaged in running after and fighting the contingent of British troops nearby. Whatever the circumstances, Odgers and his followers were not to know how many warlike Maoris they faced as they raced towards the Pah and the enemy flags, so all credit to him for leading the charge.

William Odgers remained in the Navy until 1868 when he retired to run the Union Inn in Saltash, overlooking the River Tamar and Devonport's historic naval base. He died in Saltash in December 1873.

OLVER

Derived, according to most sources, from *Golva,* 'a watch place', this name is quite distinct from Oliver, which most say is of Latin origins and means 'olive tree'. Although Oliver has more in pure numbers in Cornwall than Olver, it is also many times more common outside Cornwall than here in the Duchy, whereas Olver boasts two in every three of its holders with direct Cornish connections, hence its inclusion. Golva and its derivatives as a place name appear in several locations across Cornwall. Penolver on the Lizard peninsula is an excellent example of the meaning of the name, fitting the location as it has the Lizard Lighthouse on its cliff tops, with Lloyd's signal station close by, both watching over the shipping coming into the English Channel. That same place also has associations with Marconi's early work with radio.

Carn Olva in Sennen parish is another high point and has associations with the legendary figure of Jan Tregeagle, who was made to weave sand into rope and carry it to the top of Carn Olva. This same Jan Tregeagle is also associated with legend at Dozmary Pool on Bodmin Moor and also at Roche Rock and several other places, and seems to have been a thoroughly bad egg!

Despite place name associations in the far west, it is the east of the county where most Olver families are to be found, with well over half living in the Liskeard area and further east towards St Germans and the border with Devonshire. Indeed, one source even suggests that the name is Devonian in origin but if it is, then by 1861 most have crossed the Tamar or are as close as can be, living in the border parishes around Plymouth and Tavistock.

A look at leases and property deeds going back as far as the mid-sixteenth century confirms that the Olver name has certainly been quite widespread in Cornwall for several centuries. Not all of them have always been of good character though. For example, Jane Olver of Menheniot was sent to prison in 1831 for stealing 'two gallons of apples, valued at 6*d*, property of Richard Sobey.' Thomas Olver of Morval was sentenced in 1836 to 'six months hard labour in Bodmin gaol for stealing four geese and four barn door fowls.'

Olvers were also the victims of crime. John Ede of Warleggan stole a 'pair of scissors, property of John Olver' in 1836 and was 'transported for seven years.' Quite a harsh punishment even if you add in the theft of 'two barn door fowls, property of Hugh Coppin and four barn door fowls, property of Richard Lean.'

Back in 1780, Francis Olver of Morval had '20lbs of hay, value 2*d*' stolen by John Southern for which the accused was imprisoned for a month. Harsh punishment for crime was the order of the day in eighteenth and early nineteenth-century Cornwall.

The Olver name is also found among those who have paid the ultimate sacrifice in time of war. These include the name of Charles Henry Olver of St Germans, who lost his life at the age of twenty-nine aboard HMS *Amphion,* the first Royal Navy ship to be sunk by enemy action in the First World War on 6 August 1914. Just six weeks after the start of the war, she hit a German mine off the east coast whilst returning to Harwich.

OPIE

I have a personal interest in this one as it was my mother's maiden name. Her family were from the Stithians and Wendron areas and were mainly miners. Also, many of them worked at the former Perran Foundry at Perranarworthal. I have found the name spelt in a variety of ways. Opie is most accepted today, but there is also Oppie, Opy, Opey, Oppy, Oppey and perhaps another one or two I have not yet discovered. It all goes back to the time when earning a living was far more important than remembering ages or birthdays or learning to read and write. So it is with other family names and place names. We have many in this book which have evolved down the years. Some it seems may have been changed so much from their original form that we no longer recognise their beginnings, those where we simply have 'origin unknown' as the meaning.

Opie is perhaps one such name. Most accept that it is a derivative of the medieval personal name Osbert or Osbold, but there is nothing I can find to verify this origin. Although it is almost uniquely found in Cornwall, there seems to be no reason why an Osbert of somewhere else in England might not have given his name to a dynasty which now lives elsewhere. So why only Cornwall? Again, no answer can be given except that perhaps it is changed so much from its original form that it is not recognisable, or its original form has been lost.

Some of the oldest mentions of the Opie name here in Cornwall come from the records of the Manor of Penhargard in Helland parish near Bodmin, which was owned by an Opie family at least as far back as 1560. The manors of this area were mentioned in the *Domesday Book* and evidence exists of even earlier settlement. Penhargard Castle on this site is an Iron Age fortification, so there is evidence of human occupation dating back several millennia. The Manor of Penhargard was in the name of Sir Humphrey Stafford in 1400, who later sold it and ownership then passed through several generations of the Opie family. In a document dated 5 June 1663, Thomas Opie, gentleman of Penhargard, and Nicholas Opie of Pawton agree upon a marriage settlement when Nicholas marries Mary Opie, daughter of Thomas, so there was a joining of two related branches of the family in marriage.

The marriage not only joined distant cousins but also joined the two manors together. Often at this time marriages were 'arranged' to the financial advantage of the families rather than for 'mere true love'. This same Thomas Opie sold Penhargard to Thomas Hobly. His granddaughter married into the Peter family who became owners and it has subsequently passed on to others in more recent times. I am not able to claim any direct family association with these Bodmin Opie families, mine all seem to have been 'working class' rather than 'landed gentry', but one day I may lay claim to my Manorial Heritage!

Neither can I lay claim to being descended from the same Opie family as 'The Cornish Wonder', painter and scholar John Opie. He was born in 1761 into a working class family, his father Edward Opie being a carpenter and builder. By the age of twelve, John was excelling as a scholar to the extent that he was giving private mathematics lessons. John was encouraged by his mother, but discouraged by his father from following an artistic career, his father preferring that he join the family business. His father's will prevailed at first and John began a career as a carpenter and hated every minute of it. His local reputation as an artist soon spread as far as Truro and he was bought out of apprenticeship by Dr Wolcot, a Truro physician, who also wrote under the pen name of Peter Pendar.

He was a very colourful character, born in Devon in 1738. He had qualified as a surgeon in Aberdeen, spent time as Physician-General in Jamaica, came back and was ordained a Deacon one day and a Priest the very next day by the Bishop of London, who wanted someone to take on a potentially vacant living in Jamaica where the incumbent was thought to be dying. Pendar arrived back in Jamaica to find that the poor man had not died, and after a while in a vastly inferior living, returned again to England and to Cornwall, where he joined his uncle in medical practice in Fowey before setting up his own practice in Truro, upsetting other practitioners in the town with some of his methods.

He was challenged to a duel, became Mayor of Truro, served as the town's MP for three years and also held down an army career. He bought a house on the outskirts of Truro, tore it down and built another in its place, naming it Penmount. The site is now the local crematorium. All of this was done before he 'discovered' John Opie and introduced him to London society as 'the Cornish Wonder' in 1781. Some say that Dr Wolcot's patronage of Opie was out of a desire to see this young Cornishman succeed in a field in which he needed guidance to reach his potential; others say that Wolcot saw only a profit in the patronage. Given his track record, I would say there was at least a glint of the potential profit in his generosity.

Opie's name was soon on the lips of everyone in London and beyond. He became a close friend of Sir Joshua Reynolds, who was at the time President of the Royal Academy. The friendship and close working relationship lasted until Reynolds died in 1792. London went a little to Opie's head; he married Mary Burn, daughter of a solicitor, but it was never to be a happy union. Some years later she eloped and Opie was granted a divorce. Like most 'superstars' of every generation, his popularity faded. He remarried in 1798, and this time it seems for true love. His bride was Amelia Alderson, herself a writer and daughter of a Norwich physician, who counted Wordsworth and Sir Walter Scott among her friends. Life was on the up again and several happier years followed, during which John Opie lectured to the Royal Institution and became Professor of Painting at the Royal Academy in 1805. At the age of just forty-six he became ill and, despite the loving care of his wife, his devoted sister, Elizabeth, who travelled up from Cornwall to help nurse him in his illness and a number of noted physicians of the day, he died on 9 April 1807. He was buried in St Paul's Cathedral, alongside Sir Joshua Reynolds and a host of other great names from England's varied history, true testament to his acquired standing in the history of art and artists.

PASCOE

Over 80 per cent of England's Pascoe families are in Cornwall in the mid-nineteenth century, a percentage which has dropped from over 85 per cent in the first full census of England and Wales in 1841, and which dropped even further to just over 60 per cent by the end of the century. It was a name then which typifies the move of population from the early nineteenth century through the next hundred years, with mass emigration to find work and the beginning of the era of travel made possible by the ever expanding railway network and a better road system throughout the country.

Pascoe is derived from *Pask,* meaning 'Easter' and is found right across Cornwall, but its numbers decline the further east you go. The main concentration is in the Redruth area, where there have been

Pascoe families associated with stone masonry and quarrying in and around Stithians for many generations, right down to the present day. Several other Pascoe families around Wendron and Stithians are miners, so no surprise then that some of these turn up in later records in places like Calumet in Michigan, Grass Valley in California, Montana and Pennsylvania. Australia's mining areas also have their fair share of migrating Pascoes, and there is a Pascoe's Vale in Melbourne named after John Pascoe Fawkner, the son of a transported English convict who made a name for himself in business circles in the early days of the development of Australia. John Pascoe Fawkner's middle name came from his mother's side, as she had Cornish connections. So we can see a spread of the name worldwide from roots firmly based in Cornwall.

Another Pascoe who inherited his middle name from his mother was Francis Polkinghorne Pascoe. His father, William Pascoe, married Catherine or Kitty Polkinghorne in Madron in September 1812 and Francis was born just a year later. He was baptised in September 1813 in the Jordan Baptist Church, Penzance, also known as the Octagonal Church because of its shape. George Charles 'Bosun' Smith was minister of the church at the time. He is an interesting character in his own right. He later achieved recognition as the Seaman's Preacher and his work helped to found the Seaman's Mission, an organisation which has become known worldwide for its work with seafarers, often far from their homeland.

Francis Polkinghorne Pascoe's career took him to places far from home. He trained in medicine at St Bartholomew's Hospital, London, and thereafter joined the Navy, where he served in a variety of locations including Australia, the West Indies and the Mediterranean. He married Mary Glasson in Falmouth in 1843, but sadly Mary died in 1851. Francis, by now out of the Navy, moved to London where he concentrated full time on his life-long love of natural history, and entomology in particular. Coleoptera, beetles to you and me, were his main interest.

He went on bug hunting trips to Europe, North Africa and the Amazon region, but it seems that he was far better at dissecting them and writing about them than he was at actually catching them, and most of his work was carried out on specimens caught by others. He became a Fellow of the Entomological Society in 1854 and its President from 1864-65. He was also a member of entomological societies in France and Belgium. He became a Fellow of the Linnean Society in 1852, a society founded over 200 years ago and named after

Carl Linnaeus, the father of modern plant and animal classification, and was also a member of the Council of the Ray Society, a body formed in 1844 and dedicated to research in the field of natural sciences.

He lived for many years at 1 Burlington Road, Paddington, London with his three daughters, Flora, Kate and Maude, all of whom carried his mother's maiden name of Polkinghorne as a middle name, and none of whom it seems ever married or had an occupation, living spinster lives on their father's income.

Francis Polkinghorne Pascoe died at the age of seventy-nine on 20 June 1893.

PAYNTER

One of the earliest Paynter name references in Cornwall was in fact born William de Camborne. He killed a man by the name of William Paynter in a duel, and took not only his name but also his wife. Not an auspicious start. He was a wealthy man living at Deverill in Gwinear and was granted a coat of arms in 1569. The Paynter family are believed to have been in Gwinear since the thirteenth century, and possibly even a couple of hundred years before that to the time when William the Conqueror divided England amongst his gang of victorious noblemen and other sundry helpers.

Another estate in that part of Cornwall, Trelissick in St Erth parish, was Paynter property at least as far back as 1600, when it was held by William Paynter. One of the last of that line to live in Cornwall was John de Camborne Paynter, born in 1844. Perhaps he was named after his long distant ancestor William de Camborne? I speculate.

As we have just seen with the Pascoe name, the name of Paynter also occurs in such Cornish mining hotspots as Mineral Point, Wisconsin, and Grass Valley, California, in later American records. Back home in Cornwall there is a long line of Paynter families in St Ives with close associations with the sea as fishermen and shipwrights.

In fact, if you went down onto the quayside in St Ives any day in the middle or late nineteenth century, when the fishing boats were coming and going and asked for William Paynter, any one of half a dozen or more men could have answered your call. Several were fishermen, there was also William Paynter, fishmonger, and William Paynter who is described in a local trade directory as 'boat builder, seine owner and collector of harbour dues.'

William Paynter built fishing boats and this was a family business. He was responsible for the design of a new type of fishing boat 'the Jumbo', which was designed specifically with a very wide bottom, ideal for harbours such as St Ives where low tide leaves the boats high and dry. The wider bottom of the vessels allowed them to sit upright at low tide rather than roll over to one side with the potential for damage. Boats could also be worked on much easier if they were upright on the sand, and they also took up less space in a crowded small harbour.

These boats were also ideal for working on fishing grounds closer inshore. It was probably not an overnight flash of genius which led to the new design, more an evolving of design to suit need over a period of time. The first 'official' Jumbo was built in 1885 and by 1890 there were over twenty working in and around St Ives. The name is believed to have come from Jumbo the elephant, London Zoo's prize exhibit at the time, who was controversially sold to Barnum & Bailey's Circus in America, despite petitions of up to 10,000 names being sent by school children to Queen Victoria. Sadly Jumbo the elephant had a shorter life even than the class of fishing boat named after him. He was killed when hit by a train in 1885.

The fishing industry was hit by changing times and unfortunately for William Paynter was in severe decline by the end of the nineteenth century. The first years of the new century saw the ending of the need for his new boats and within another twenty years, most had been broken up or sold.

In very recent times the Jumbo class has been revitalised and rebuilt, and it is pleasing to report that a design of fishing boats, almost extinct for nearly a hundred years, is again now sailing St Ives Bay.

PELLOW

—◊◊◊—

Sometimes spelt Pellew or with an 'e' on the end, there are two schools of thought as to the origin of this name. The first is that it came across with William the Conqueror, as did so many of our English names, and that it is from the region of Belleau, meaning 'good water', in France, an area south and east of Paris which saw a major battle between German and

American troops in June 1918. The second, and the Cornish connection, is that is comes from Pell, meaning 'far off', so perhaps folk who lived by a good water supply or those who lived far away from the main settlement. As with other names it has to be said that its majority presence in this small corner of England we call Cornwall would indicate a Celtic origin rather than one which came across with any invader, which you might expect to find widespread across the whole country.

The name is spread across Cornwall from Penzance to Launceston but the main stronghold is in the Falmouth area within the parishes of Mabe, Budock and Mawnan. Despite this close proximity to the sea, most of the Pellow families from this area are farmers rather than engaged in seafaring trades. The Pellew spelling seems to be mainly confined to the Penzance area with a scattering elsewhere. Bear in mind though that this distribution of the spelling interpretation of any name is mainly in the hands of the census enumerator and his version in Penzance and that of his counterpart in Falmouth or Launceston may have been different. Calling from door to door they had little time to seek clarification of spelling, even if the householders knew the correct spelling themselves.

One Pellew who made a name for himself was Edward Pellew, 1st Viscount Exmouth. He was born in April 1757 in Dover, the second son of Samuel Pellew, commander of a Dover packet ship, but the family roots were firmly set in Flushing, just across the water from Falmouth where Edward's grandfather, Humphrey Pellew, himself the son of a naval officer, was a merchant and ship owner. Humphrey Pellew and Samuel Trefusis were mainly responsible for the building of Flushing as a town and port. In its time it rivalled and even outshone Falmouth. The Pellew family also had interests in an American tobacco plantation in Maryland and their estate lands stood where the town of Annapolis now stands. The family moved from Flushing to Penzance when Edward's father died in 1764, but Edward stayed behind and received an education at the Truro Grammar School, that ancient seat of learning attended by so many of Cornwall's great names. Humphrey Davy, who invented the miner's safety lamp, Goldsworthy Gurney, among whose achievements were early steam carriages, Henry Martin, the missionary who translated parts of the Bible into several eastern languages, and Samuel Foote, actor and playwright, all attended the school.

Education and Edward did not see eye to eye. He is described as aggressive and confrontational and at the age of fourteen he ran away to sea as a midshipman. His temperament soon saw him in trouble and he was put ashore in Marseilles for arguing with his captain over disciplinary procedures. He was left to find his own passage back to England on another ship. His early career is notable by his actions in American waters at the Battle of Valcour Island. Promotion quickly followed and he soon had his own command. By 1804 he was Rear Admiral, and in 1816 he became 1st Viscount Exmouth and was Port Admiral at Plymouth from 1817 to 1820. When he retired from active naval service, he became a regular speaker at the House of Lords as well as keeping an eye on naval matters. In 1832 he was appointed Vice Admiral of the United Kingdom and the list of other honours bestowed upon him both in England and abroad is quite extensive.

Despite all this he found time to marry Susannah Frowde and they had six children, four sons and two daughters. The eldest son, Pownoll Bastard Pellew inherited the title and became 2nd Viscount Exmouth. The second son, Fleetwood Broughton Reynolds Pellew, followed the family naval tradition, later becoming an admiral and being knighted. The third son, George, was to become Dean of Norwich and the fourth, Edward William, also followed a career in the church.

The name of Edward Pellew still lives on right across the world, with Sir Edward Pellew Islands in the Gulf of Carpentaria off the north coast of Australia named in his honour by the explorer Matthew Flinders. Cape Pellew is close by, as is Exmouth Gulf. On the other side of the world there is also Pellew Island off the coast of Jamaica and even further afield, Point Pellew to the north of Prince William Sound, Alaska. Some sources also say that Palau, formerly the Pelew Islands in the Philippines, is also named after him, but the name was there before Edward Pellew came to prominence, and is more likely to be an English version of the local name Belau.

Edward Pellew died at his home at Bitton House, Teignmouth, Devon in January 1833 at the age of seventy-six.

PENALUNA

There are about 140 Penaluna names on the census of 1861, of which all but a small handful are living in Cornwall, with all having Cornish places of birth. How much more Cornish can you get? Narrow it down a little more and you have some 60 per cent of Penalunas born in the parish of Wendron, near Helston. As might be expected living in this area, there is a fair sprinkling of miners amongst them, leading to the name occurring later in the nineteenth century in the usual mining haunts of the Cornish, like Nevada, Michigan and southern Australia. There are also a few who travelled to other mining areas such as the coal mines of Durham and Yorkshire and the lead mines of North Wales.

The name has two possible origins, *Pen* certainly means 'end of', 'top of' or 'head of', but different sources give either *Lynoww,* meaning 'ponds' or 'pools', or *Lonnow,* meaning 'grove of bushes' as the origin of the second part. Again it is a name with distinct Cornishness, with plenty of references going back many centuries, but with a very small distribution area.

The manor of Pennalun is mentioned in the Domesday Survey of 1086. Historians suggest this could be Penaluna in Veryan or Penhallam in Jacobstow, but whichever has the greater claim, it is evidence of the age of the name.

One Penaluna on the 1861 census is of interest. William Penaluna, born in Stithians in 1780, spent some time in his early years in London and on his return to Cornwall in the early 1800s, he advertised his business as 'engaged in the sale of pens, books, prints, soaps, trinkets, musical instruments, patent medicines, pickles and clothes.' A true 'general merchant'. He was also briefly in partnership with John Heard, founder of the *West Briton.* The two men opened a printing office in Falmouth but the partnership was short-lived, Heard moved to Truro where he continued to publish his newspaper, whilst Penaluna moved on to Helston where he spent the rest of his life.

He signed a fourteen-year lease on 23 December 1807 for premises at Meneage Street, in the ownership of Richard Gerveys Grylls, a man we have met before under his own family name, at a rate of £47 5s per annum. This was quite a sum and equivalent today to around £1,600, so he must have been expecting to make a tidy income.

He took over the printing of *Lean's Engine Reporter* in 1811, a specialist periodical devoted to 'the comparative duty of the mine engines in Cornwall'. By 1817 he was declared bankrupt, mainly because of publication delays of a book entitled *A History of Cornwall,* which was due to be published in 1816 but finally hit the streets in 1824. In 1817 he published *The Circle or Historical Survey of Sixty Parishes and Towns.* William Penaluna also became a printer and publisher of 'broadside ballads'. These were popular songs of the day, printed as broadsheets, sold and pinned up in various places like shops and market places so that ordinary folk could read them and learn the words. They first appeared as far back as the sixteenth century and their popularity lasted until the early years of the twentieth century, when other means of mass publicity of new songs, like radio, came along and spelt the end of the trade.

Penaluna married in 1836, his bride a widow named Elizabeth Lemin who, according to census records, was originally from Cork in Ireland. Some sources suggest this is an error but if it is, then it is consistent, as she shows herself as being Irish in the 1851, 1861 and 1871 census records.

By 1856, William Penaluna is described in *Kelly's Trade Directory* as 'Bookseller, Bookbinder, Printer, Stationer and Agent to the Minerva Life and Sun Fire & Life Assurance Companies', with an address still in Meneage Street, Helston. He died in Helston in 1864. His widow, Elizabeth, continued to live in Helston where she died at the age of eighty-six in 1880.

PENBERTHY

If you have Penberthy blood in your veins, then the chances are that your roots lie in the west of Cornwall, as most folk of that name are to be found in and around the parishes of St Ives, Lelant and Ludgvan. The name is derived from *Pen,* meaning 'end', 'top' or 'head of', and *Perthy,* meaning 'bushes'. One of my personal favourite places, especially out of the holiday season is Penberth Cove at Treen, just a few miles from Land's End. There is nearly always a black cat roaming around the quayside whenever you visit, waiting it seems for the fishing boats to come home. This tranquil spot derives its name from the same source, as does Penperth on the Roseland Peninsula near King Harry Ferry.

PENGELLY

Another name which has *Pen* as a prefix, this time with *Kelly* meaning 'copse' or 'grove', so 'the folks who lived at the end of the copse' or 'top of the grove of trees'. It is one of many names which evolved as descriptions of where people lived. As a place name, Pengelly is found in many places across Cornwall, from Delabole in the north east down to the Penzance area. As a family name it is equally well spread from Stratton to Sancreed.

When it comes to selecting a short biography, there are several to choose from. Again, one involves the sinking of the *Titanic*. Frederick William Pengelly was born in 1892 in Tavistock to a Cornish mining family, and later moved back across the border and lived in Chilsworthy, near Gunnislake. Like William Henry Nancarrow and Stephen Curnow Jenkin, who have previously been mentioned under the entries for their surnames, it is said that Pengelly was aboard the *Titanic* only by fate. His voyage had been booked on another ship but because of a coal workers' strike, that ship did not sail, so he transferred to the *Titanic*. He was destined for Butte, Montana where he and three travelling companions were to join other Cornish miners, but none ever arrived.

Another notable bearer of the name isSir Thomas Pengelly, 1675–1730, who was a Judge and Chief Baron of the Exchequer in the reign of George I, and his portrait hangs in the National Gallery in London.

The Pengelly name is also to be found as a prominent family name across the border in Devon, where the family owned the estate of Sortridge near Peter Tavy in the seventeenth and eighteenth centuries, having purchased it from the Glanville family.

Another Pengelly born in Cornwall but remembered more for his work in neighbouring Devon was William Pengelly. Born in Looe in 1812, he was the son of a sea captain and a member of a Looe family with generations of seafaring and fishing experience before and after his time. He left his schooling at the age of twelve and joined his father at sea. He was a widely and mainly self-educated man and in his mid-twenties left the sea to concentrate on a career teaching mathematics. A move to Torquay in 1836 saw him open a day school there, teaching by the fashionable Pestalozzian method, a progressive teaching technique pioneered by the Swiss teacher, Jean Henri Pestalozzi. By the late 1840s, his interests had switched to science and he published a paper in 1849 on the subject of fossilised fish which he had discovered on a beach in his home town of Looe. His main work was back in Torquay where he continued the work of Father John MacEnery in excavating human remains from Kent's Caverns. MacEnery's findings of ancient fossils, bones and other fragments had caused great concern to him as a Catholic priest, and others in the Church, as it directly challenged the Bible's version of creation. It was also at around this time that Darwin was also questioning the origins of our species.

Fortunately for Pengelly, by the time he began his work, there was a more liberal attitude in some circles towards the beginnings of the human race and he went on to publish over a hundred scientific papers and articles relating to geology, palaeontology and man's evolution. He founded the Torquay Natural History Society and the Devonshire Association for the Advancement of Literature, Science and Art to spread the findings of his work with others of a like mind. He married Mary Ann Mudge in 1838 and they had three children. Sadly Mary died in 1851, but William remarried in 1853 to Lydia Spriggs, daughter of a Quaker family originally from Worcestershire. They had two daughters, Lydia and Hester, and his wife later wrote his biography. William Pengelly died on 16 March 1894 at his home near Torquay.

PENROSE

Again we have the *Pen* prefix, this time with *Ros* meaning 'heathland' added to it, and like the other 'Pen' names we have noted above, this too is an ancient name here in Cornwall. The oldest reference I can find is to Philip de Penros, in the Pipe Rolls of Cornwall dated 1195. Pipe rolls were kept by the Crown from as early as 1130 and were, in simplest form, the forerunner to the Inland Revenue, collecting taxes on behalf of the Crown. In 1411 John Penrose was Member of Parliament for Liskeard and in 1527, Henry Penrose became Lord Lieutenant of Cornwall, so a family with a long pedigree and many distinguished members down several centuries. However, unlike some names we have seen which have stayed in a very small area of Cornwall, the name of Penrose is to be found right across England by the middle of the nineteenth century, with quite a gathering of the clan in Yorkshire. A few of these have moved from Cornwall for mining work, but by far the majority are at least second or third generation Yorkshire born and bred. Why is a genuine Cornish Celtic name found so far north? Possibly a mining connection but other than that, I have no explanation.

Back in Cornwall, most nineteenth-century Penrose families are to be found in the middle and west of the county, although there are few east of a line drawn from Falmouth through Truro and across to St Agnes.

One Penrose, born in Penryn in 1759, was Charles Vinicombe Penrose, second son of John Penrose, who was vicar of St Gluvias for some thirty-five years and his wife, Elizabeth, formerly Vinicombe. Unlike his father and maternal grandfather, who was also a churchman, Charles decided upon a career at sea, joining the Royal Academy for naval cadets at Portsmouth at the age of just thirteen. In 1775 he joined his first ship under the watchful eye of Captain the Hon. George Murray. He served in the Mediterranean, English Channel and North Sea where he assisted in the capture of several French vessels. In 1779 he was promoted to the rank of lieutenant and transferred to HMS *Cleopatra,* again under Captain Murray. Penrose saw action in several locations during the next few years including Spanish, French and West Indian waters.

By 1794 he had become Captain Penrose, his first command being HMS *Lynx*. He was sent to Bermuda to carry out hydrographical studies for a new harbour and very nearly lost his ship in a storm on the way back to England. Penrose then rejoined the now Vice-Admiral Murray on HMS *Resolution* and served with him for several years before being promoted again to Commodore in 1810, in charge of naval operations in Gibraltar. He became Rear Admiral just three years later and was awarded the KCB, Knight Commander of the Order of the Bath in 1816. This same year he saw action in Algiers with another naval man of Cornish blood who we have previously met, Edward Pellew, 1st Viscount Exmouth. In 1821 he became Vice Admiral Penrose. When his long and distinguished naval career came to an end, he retired to Ethy, near Lostwithiel, where he died in 1830.

POLKINGHORNE

—⁓—

There is a Cornish Polkinghorne family in London on the 1861 census, one in Portsmouth and an Inspector Polkinghorne in HM Dockyard Police in Devonport. Add to these a couple of other Cornish Polkinghorne named shown as 'at sea' and a couple of other 'strays', and you have the sum total of those not living in Cornwall. It is a Cornish name, the *Pol* being 'pool', 'cove' or 'creek' and the second part is derived from *Kynhorn*, meaning 'iron chief', giving a full meaning of 'the pool of the iron chief.'

Sithney, Crowan, Gwinear and Illogan, four parishes spanning the width of west Cornwall, have a majority of Cornwall's Polkinghorne families and most of these, as might be expected for this area, are miners. As we have seen with other Cornish mining names, the Polkinghorne name has, by the end of the nineteenth century, spread to the mining areas of Keweenaw and Mineral Point in North America as well as to Ontario, Canada, and several locations in Australia and New Zealand.

The oldest record of the name which I can find here in Cornwall comes from 1299 in Gwinear parish, where the Polkinghorne estate is in the ownership of Roger de Polkinghorne, who was granted a coat of arms by Edward lll, described as 'Three bars Sable with a Crest of an Arm in Armour, embowed, holding a Battleaxe'. Quite suitable for an 'iron chief'. Polkinghorne Manor as a place name can still be found on modern maps of the area, just to the north of Gwinear village. The estate and the right to the family arms was held up to the time of Otho Polkinghorne in the mid-seventeenth century. His heiress, Mary, married Thomas Glynn of Helston, another long established Cornish family whose roots were in the Glynn estate just east of Bodmin, and the Polkinghorne estate passed to the Glynn family by this marriage. A later marriage between the Glynn and Grylls families of Helston we have already noted under the entry for the Grylls family. This transfer of property from one family to another through marriage was a common theme amongst many of the 'landed gentry' down many centuries, and ensured that large estates stayed within this merry band of a small handful of families.

The Polkinghorne name, sometimes found without the 'e' on the end, is quite widespread across Cornwall by the seventeenth century. The 1641 Protestation Returns list a total of nearly thirty Polkinghorn names from Mullion, St Keverne and Penzance in the west through Gwinear and Crowan up to Merther, Probus and St Stephen further east.

Perhaps the one Polkinghorne best known in Cornwall was James Polkinghorne. Born in St Keverne, he later became landlord of the Red Lion Inn, St Columb. He was a champion Cornish wrestler, who beat everyone who came to challenge him, even the great Richard Parkyn of St Mawgan. James Polkinghorne is described as having 'the neck of a bull, curly hair, a piercing stare and determined jaw, weighing 230lbs and standing six feet two' in one short biography.

His greatest moment came on 23 October 1826, when a challenge match between Cornwall and Devon saw him take on Abram Cann, champion of Devon. The match took place at Tamar Green, Moricetown, Devonport, for a purse of £200 a man for the 'best of three back falls'. It was the subject of much discussion and controversy even before it began. The rules of wrestling were rather different in the two counties and so had to be arbitrated upon before the contest. Accounts vary, depending on which side of the Tamar you look, but the agreement finally reached was that the Devon rules be used, which allowed Cann to wear his 'heavy boots with the toes soaked in bullocks blood and then baked', a considerable advantage over a bare footed opponent! As many as 12,000 'hollorin' fans watched the contest as first Polkinghorne won a fall and then Cann threw his opponent. One fall was hotly disputed and settled by the toss of a coin in favour of Polkinghorne... imagine a football referee these days deciding a controversial Premier League goal by tossing a coin! In the end the contest was declared a draw, and a plaque commemorating the event can still be found on the wall of the Red Lion Inn, St Columb.

QUICK

A name which by every source is given the meaning of 'wooded valley', from *Gwyk,* or one of several variants of that spelling. If you have Quick blood in your veins then the chances are that your family was originally from the area around St Ives and the coastal parishes of Zennor and Towednack to the west. There are not too many wooded valleys in this part of Cornwall to give provenance to the origin of the name, more rocky crags and high windswept cliffs, but it is an area where, on nineteenth-century census records, at least two out of every three family members say they were born. The Quick families of this area are all said to be descended from a mariner who was shipwrecked at Wicca Pool in Zennor in 1470.

One such descendant was John Quick, born at Trevassa in Towednack parish in 1852. His father was a farmer, also named John, who in 1854 decided to try his hand at farming and gold prospecting in the newly emerging colony of Victoria, Australia. The family settled in Bendigo, along with many other Cornish families, but tragedy was to befall them when John senior died just a few months after arriving in their new homeland. His widow, Mary, remarried another Cornishman by the name of Vine. John junior received a basic education but left his schooling at the age of just ten and began working in an iron foundry in Long Gully before joining the *Bendigo Evening News* and later the *Bendigo Independent* as a junior reporter. He moved to Melbourne where he attended university and qualified as a Bachelor of Law, but instead of pursuing a career in the legal profession, he continued in journalism, taking an ever increasing interest in politics. In 1880 he was elected as a Member of the Parliament of Victoria, representing his home area of Bendigo. In 1882 he became Doctor of Law and in 1883 he married Catherine Harris, daughter of another family with Cornish connections. 1889 saw him lose his seat in the Victorian Assembly and this could have been the end of his political career, but he and a handful of others were by now airing the view that Australia should become a unified federation, rather than several self-governing states.

Some dismissed the idea and debate and discussion took place over the next decade before, on 1 January 1901, the new Australian Federation was inaugurated. John Quick became Sir John Quick at the same time, in recognition of his services to the federal movement. His book, *The Annotated Constitution of the Australian Commonwealth*, jointly published with another pioneer of a united Australia, Robert Garran, is still considered to be one of the best and most authoritative works on that country's constitution. Garran was a legal expert, widely accepted as the foremost constitutional expert of his generation, who became the first employee of the new Government of Australia, being appointed Solicitor General.

Next door to Towednack is the parish of Zennor, famous for its mermaid who lured church chorister Matthew Trewella to the deep. His singing to her can still be heard, they say, in Pendour Cove. But legend aside Zennor Church has reason to remember the name of Quick. There is a sundial on the tower wall inscribed, 'The Glory of the World Paseth', with the name and date, 'Paul Quick, 11 February 1737'.

A couple of Quick generations later we find the name of Henry Quick in the baptism register of Zennor in December 1792. He was named after his father, who had married Margery George in nearby Paul, in January of the same year. Henry was a 'sickly child', prone to fits and not able to work the land or go down the mines like most of the boys of the area. His father died when he was just twelve years old and he and his mother struggled to earn enough to keep themselves from the workhouse. Often to be found begging on the streets, their lives were quite miserable until Henry's gift of writing poetry began to bring in a few pennies. He wrote poems and went around the streets of the local towns and villages ringing a bell to call out anyone

The sundial clock on the wall of Zennor Church, inscribed 'The Glory of the World Paseth' with the name and date, 'Paul Quick, 11 February 1737'.

wishing to part with their hard earned pennies to hear one of his works. His mother died in 1832. Henry had not previously married but at the age of forty-three he married a widow, Jane Rowe, who at sixty-seven was old enough to be his mother. She, like many others, believed that he had become wealthy from sales of his poems and that he had a fortune stashed away somewhere, and this seems to have been the sole basis for her interest in the marriage. Sadly she was mistaken and the marriage was not a happy one. The 1841 census shows the couple, with his wife shown as Jenepher, aged seventy-four and Henry as forty-eight, living at Mill Downs, Zennor. The entry in the occupation column for Henry says 'Rhymes'. Among his rhymes was his own autobiographical poem entitled *The Life and Progress of Henry Quick of Zennor*. First written in 1843, he revised it in 1851. Among its 400 or more lines is the verse:

> Eight years of tedious grief and strife,
> I've suffered with a jealous wife,
> Her discontent torments me sore,
> Suspicious I have paltry store.

Henry Quick died on 9 October 1857 and is buried in Zennor churchyard.

RETALLACK

This is another name describing the place of abode of some of its original owners and again it is a name with two equally sound versions of its origin. *Res* is 'a ford on a river', no problem there, but *Talek* is a 'steep slope', whilst *Helec* or *Helyk* is 'willow wood'. Both are given with equal confidence as the origin by different scholars who have studied the subject of the Cornish Celtic language, and again I have no proof to offer to side with either as the true origin. Yet another suggestion is that is comes from *Talawg,* which means 'high forehead', or even from *Attal,* an ancient name given to alluvial tin streams in Cornwall, but the majority side with one or other of the first two suggestions. It certainly qualifies as a Cornish name with over 85 per cent being found in Cornwall or of direct Cornish origin. Some of the oldest references to the name can be found in the Arundell archives, and the accounts of Lady Joan Arundell dating back to 1387, when John Talek was Reeve of Arundell lands at Penpol. A reeve was an elected official whose job it was to ensure the smooth running of an estate on behalf of the Lord of the Manor. It was a very old system dating back to Saxon times.

Bodmin, St Austell and St Columb are strongholds of the name. Retallack as a place name can be found in several locations across Cornwall, including Winnard's Perch near St Columb and in St Hilary parish near Penzance. Retallack in St Hilary was owned by the Agar-Robartes family of the Lanhydrock estate until parts of their estates were auctioned off in 1912. The auction catalogue mentions 'a tenement known as Retallack, in the occupation of John Pearce'. It was sold for £200.

But the place name of Retallack is by no means confined to Cornwall. If you are the sort who really wants to get away from it all, take a trip to Retallack, British Columbia. This deserted old mining town is about 200 miles west of Calgary, high in the coastal mountain ranges between the Rocky Mountains and Vancouver. In the nineteenth century it was the centre of the local mining industry, today it is almost totally deserted except for a small handful of the hardiest skiers in winter. Proof, if ever it were needed, that Cornwall's mining influence has spread to even the remotest corners of the world.

RODDA

—⁓—

Again this is very much a west Cornwall name, proof again perhaps of William Bottrell's theory about West Penwith which we looked at in our introduction and 'its almost insular position, one of the most secluded and unknown parts of England.'

As for a meaning, one source suggests the old English word of *Roda,* meaning 'a clearing in a forest', but there are few forests in West Penwith to support this theory! Others suggest a personal name, whilst others are happy to suggest 'origin obscure', as we have with some previous names. Perhaps we have another name which is so far removed from its original form that we can not see the wood for the trees... a clearing in the forest may be needed to help! Whatever the

origins, about 80 per cent of England's Victorian Rodda population
are west of a line from Helston through Redruth to the north coast.

Today there is one particular product in Cornwall which everyone
associates with the name of Rodda, clotted cream, but back in the
nineteenth century, a lot of Roddas were mining families around
Crowan, Breage and further west around St Just in Penwith. There
are also Rodda names to be found in the St Just area, running small
businesses. Grocers, tailors, drapers and dressmakers all feature. Some of
the oldest surviving records of the Rodda name come from leases and
deeds dating from the middle of the seventeenth century in places such
as Gulval and Madron. The Cornwall Quarter Sessions records also
show that not all Roddas have always been of good character. Mary
Rodda of Gulval was brought before the magistrates in 1799 for 'being
of disorderly conduct in the Workhouse', whilst Stephen Rodda, miller
of Gulval, appears at least three times between 1758 and 1769 accused of
'assault and battery', and a couple of non-specific misdemeanours. He
was fined on each occasion having confessed to his crimes. For stealing
'two pairs of trousers and two yards of cloth', in 1826, Martin Rodda of
Kenwyn received 'twelve months in Bodmin gaol with hard labour'.

ROSEVEAR

Most agree that this name is derived from *Ros*, meaning 'heathland'
or 'uncultivated land', and *Vur,* meaning 'large' or 'great', so 'folk who
lived on or near a large area of uncultivated land or heathland', of which
we have quite a lot in Cornwall. Rosevear near Bugle, for example, is
in an area of heathland and although now almost entirely surrounded
by china clay works, it is quite easy to see that the translation of the
place name fits the location. Most of Cornwall's Rosevear families are
also to be found in the St Austell area with St Austell itself being a
favoured location and adjacent parishes such as St Ewe and Luxulyan
also contribute to the numbers.

We have just met a remote Canadian location with a Cornish name in
Retallack and here is another. Rosevear, Alberta, is about 130 miles west
of Edmonton in the foothills of the Rocky Mountains. Like Retallack,
Rosevear is now a name on the map rather than the thriving community
it once was, and its population is now given as 'nil'. The town and the

area around it thrived with the coming of the Grand Trunk Pacific Railway, which ran from near Thunder Bay on Lake Superior down through Edmonton and Jasper and on through the Rocky Mountains to the Pacific coast at Port Fraser, British Columbia. It formed part of a rail link right across Canada from the Atlantic to the Pacific.

Closer to home, the name of Rosevear is associated with sea tragedy. In February 1784, whilst on passage from India back to England, the mail packet ship *Nancy* was lost amid the jagged snares of the Western Rocks of Scilly. She was under the command of Captain Hildane and among the passengers was his lover, singer and actress Ann Cargill. She and other passengers took to the lifeboats but sad to say there was only one survivor. Ann Cargill's body, dressed in her nightwear, was found still clutching a baby in her arms. The bodies of the poor souls lost in the wreck were buried on nearby Rosevear Island. This same island was used about a hundred years later as a base for workmen constructing the Bishop Rock lighthouse. It is said that they were haunted by the singing voice of a woman, believed to be the ghost of Ann Cargill. Even today legend tells that Ann's voice can still be heard and that the ghostly figure of a woman wearing her night attire still walks the small, barren Rosevear Island.

ROWSE

The name of Rowse or Rouse is found quite evenly spread right across Cornwall. It is derived from *Ros,* meaning 'heathland' as we have just seen in the name of Rosevear, although there is a source which offers the suggestion that it might be from the French *Rous,* for 'redhead'. I prefer the Celtic derivation, as accepted in most quarters.

In choosing a short biography for this name, the one outstanding Rowse is of course, Alfred Leslie Rowse, born in St Austell in 1903. He was of a poor working class family but he managed to gain a place at St Austell Grammar School and from there he went on to Christ Church, Oxford, in 1921. He graduated in 1925 and his reputation grew from there. That same year he was elected a Fellow of All Souls College, Oxford. In 1927 he was became a lecturer at Merton College and two years later he was awarded a Master of Arts degree. In 1931 he turned to politics and unsuccessfully challenged as Labour candidate for the

Falmouth and Penryn parliamentary seat. He took a post at the London School of Economics following this defeat, but stood again for Parliament in 1935. Political ambitions seem to have ended here. His writing career had begun some years before and by the end of the 1930s he had many titles to his name on historical and political subjects. Over the next five decades, Rowse continued to write on subjects as diverse as Shakespeare and cats, but perhaps his best known works are on Cornwall and the Cornish. Books like *The Cornish in America, Cornish Childhood* and *A Cornishman at Oxford*, as well as his poems on Cornish subjects, are all classics. He was, without doubt, one of Cornwall's greatest sons. He lived well into his nineties and died on 3 October 1997.

RULE

—⁓—

If you are a Rule, or have Rule blood in your family line, then there is an excellent chance that your roots lie deep in a mineshaft in the heartland of Cornish mining around Camborne and Redruth. Two-thirds of Cornwall's Rule families are to be found here in mid-Victorian times, with even larger proportions the further back you go in census records and other data. The name here derives from *Ryual* meaning 'powerful king'. It is also a name very much associated with Scotland. In the year AD 347, St Rule, a missionary, is credited with bringing the relics of St Andrew from Greece to Scotland. He was instructed to deliver his precious cargo 'to the west, in the utmost part of the world'. He was shipwrecked on the east coast of Scotland, close to the modern day town of St Andrews. Whether this was his intended final destination or whether there was more to the ancient 'west' than known to seafaring man, we may never know, but the rest, as they say, is history.

Returning to the Rule family of Cornwall, many of them have made a name for themselves in far distant places where they have gone to help develop the mining resources of their chosen destination. One such area is Mexico, where the name of Rule is synonymous with the silver mining industry. As early as 1824 we have already noted that a shipment of mining machinery was exported from the Fox Perran Foundry to Real de Monte in Mexico, and it was here and in Pachuca that the name of Rule is to be found playing a major role in the development and management of the silver mining industry.

The name of John Rule is to be found in the 1820s and 1830s and in these times of a great deal of local unrest, he argued from his position in mine management and local government that Cornish miners should be armed for their own protection. Richard Rule is credited with bringing Methodism to the area around 1840, the local population finding his teachings and the hymns they sang very different from their Catholic upbringing. Perhaps the most famous of the Rule clan in Mexico was Francis Rule. He arrived in Mexico around 1858 and became one of the wealthiest men in Mexico over the next few decades. He is credited with the discovery of the Santa Gertrudis vein of silver, one of the richest ever found in Mexico, and by the turn of the century, he was a multi-millionaire and the company was paying dividends to shareholders running into millions of dollars. Known locally as *El Ray de la Plata*, 'The Silver King', he was as generous as he was wealthy and gave back much of his wealth to the area which had made him a rich man. In 1906 when the American Smelting & Refining Company bought out much of the local silver industry, Francis Rule was manager of no less than 106 mines. His wealth was increased even more when in 1914 his companies began to exploit the Purisima vein of silver, which reached down around two-thirds of a mile deep underground, and was set to become the single most productive vein of silver ever discovered in the world. The clock tower and many civic buildings in Pachuca and the surrounding area are lasting memories to the Rule family name.

SARA

This is a name which, like others we have seen, is almost unique to Cornwall and has been here for several centuries at least, but for which there is no obvious source. 'Origin obscure' is the best that most sources will offer, but one source suggests it is from St Saire in Normandy and came across with William the Conqueror. Again, I would challenge this, as it is unlikely to have stayed in such a confined corner of the country as Cornwall if it was the name of one of the barons who were rewarded with huge chunks of England after the Battle of Hastings. I think that it is again a name which has evolved so much from its original source as to be unrecognisable.

Most Cornish Sara families are in the Falmouth area, with the adjoining parishes of Perranarworthal and Mylor being the heartland of the name, and in this area the name of Sara is very closely associated with several local iron foundries and engineering works. The Sara family involvement with this type of employment began at the Fox Perran Foundry, set up by Robert Were Fox, a name we have met before, in 1791. Records suggest that there were Sara family members employed at Perran Foundry from its earliest days. One of these, Stephen Sara, whose father and grandfather had both worked at Perran Foundry, moved on to set up his own foundry business in Penryn, and this remained in the family for two or three more generations. It is believed that Stephen Sara was the last surviving former Fox Perran Foundry apprentice at the time of his death in 1933.

Sara personnel at Perran Foundry around 1870 included Evan Sara working in the fitting shop. He is later shown on census records as 'iron founder's clerk'. Two of his sons carried on the family involvement with iron founding and engineering in Penryn and a third son moved away to Bristol.

Nicholas Sara was in the smith's shop for many years in the mid-nineteenth century, as was his son, George. Another Nicholas Sara was the original foreman of the pattern shop at Perran. The name of William Sara, born in Mylor in 1811, is to be found employing a dozen or more men and boys at his iron foundry on the Portreath road in Redruth during the second half of the nineteenth century. This, like several others in the area, was smaller than Perran, which ranked alongside Harvey's of Hayle as the two largest in Cornwall, but the smaller foundries were no less important for providing the machinery, engines and boilers used in Cornwall's mining industry. With the demise of Cornwall's mining industry, many of these men and their machines were to be found in other mining areas of the world.

SPARGO

The oldest surviving written record I have discovered of this name is *Spergour*, as far back as 1318 in the area around Mabe, near Penryn, and according to every reliable source the name comes from *Spern Cor*, meaning 'thorn hedge'. That same area still has many Spargo families in Victorian times and many of them are stone masons. Quarrying, stone masonry, stone cutting and other associated trades are common in this area where granite has been quarried for many centuries for all manner of uses, from humble gate posts to the core stone of Truro Cathedral and some of London's great bridges and buildings.

One man from Mabe who initially trained as a stone mason was John Spargo, born in 1876, the son of Thomas Spargo, also a stone mason, and his wife, Jane. The couple had married in 1874. Just to complicate the family tree a little more, Jane's maiden name was also Spargo; she was the second of ten children of John and Jane Spargo. Her father was landlord of the New Inn at Mabe for many years. John's paternal grandfather provided a third successive generation on that side of the Spargo family who were stone masons.

In addition to his work as a stone mason, John trained as a Methodist Lay Preacher and became increasingly interested in the work of Henry Hyndman. Born in London in 1842, the son of a wealthy businessman, Hyndman received a private early education, followed up at Trinity College, Cambridge, where he represented Cambridge University, the MCC and Sussex at cricket. It's not the sort of background you might expect for a man who would go on to be founder of the Social Democratic Federation and the National Socialist Party. Both he and young John Spargo were influenced in their politics by the writings of Karl Marx. Spargo was in New York by 1901 and in 1909 moved to Vermont. One of his earliest works was *The Bitter Cry of Children*, written in 1906, exposing the poor treatment of child workers in the coal mining industry of America. He later wrote on a variety of political themes, his titles including *The Jews and American Ideals, The Psychology of Bolshevism,* and *Marxism, Socialism and Religion.*

In addition to his political activities he became an avid collector of Bennington pottery, which has been made in this area since the days of the American Revolution. Spargo researched his subject very deeply and wrote two very authoritative histories, *Early American Pottery and China* and *The Potters and Potteries of Bennington*, in which he writes 'many of my personal friends have been surprised to find me interested in old cracked pots and dishes.' Pottery and politics may indeed seem two extreme interests, but he pursued both with equal vigour. He became leader of the Socialist Party of America, but left in 1917, disagreeing with the party's stance against the First World War which was then raging in Europe. He joined the National Party, but this was all but disbanded following disappointing election results in

1918. His main income came from his writing but his twin interest of ceramics also saw him as Curator of the Bennington, Vermont Historical Museum. Among his later works was an authoritative history of his own family name of Spargo, in which he suggests from his own research that the family name and the place name of Spargo in Mabe parish, which can still be found to this day near the parish church, has been in existence since about AD 400. I bow to his superior knowledge of his own family name and I am quite happy to accept his findings.

TEAGUE

I did a family history research project some time ago where I found that the name of Teague was written down by a former Methodist Minister of Carharrack as Tyack, way back in the early days of Methodism in Cornwall. It was checked, cross-referenced with census data and other sources and found to be one and the same family. At the time this caused some consternation as it changed the whole family tree from then down to the present day. Looking at the origin of the names, Teague is generally accepted as coming from *Tek* meaning 'fair' whilst Tyack comes from *Tyak,* meaning 'farmer' or 'peasant'. So it seems that my Methodist Minister may have got it wrong and, like so many back then, he took what he heard, which sounded similar to a name he had perhaps come across before, and wrote it down. Being just an average working class mining family, those whose children were receiving his baptismal blessing could not read nor write their own names, and so could not correct his apparent error. The Teague name in Victorian census records is found in many parts of Cornwall and further afield in England, but its main concentration is in the Redruth area where, as would be expected, many are mining families. The name is now worldwide, with many to be found in the usual haunts of the Cornish miner, but evidence also exists to confirm that even before the mining exodus that Teagues were settling in early Virginia and other early American east coast colonies as long as 350 years ago. Whether they were all from Cornwall is not clear but it is certainly a possibility, as many of the early settlements on the eastern coast of America had concentrations of mariners, fishermen and early settlers from this part of England. One such was Edward Teague, who sailed from Bristol in 1655 to settle in Cecil County, Maryland, where he purchased 290 acres of land and named it Teague's Delight.

The name of Teague is also found in Ireland and many of these families were also among the early settlers in America.

TIPPETT

A name which most agree is derived from the Germanic name Theobold, meaning 'bold people'. This name is not exclusively Cornish but there is a sufficient percentage of them within Cornwall to suggest that it belongs here rather than anywhere else in the country. It is found quite widely across Cornwall and, unlike some names we have seen, it has no particular geographical limitations or locations.

Employment in Tippet families also covers a wide spectrum from mining and farming through to shoemakers, tailors and Edward Tippett, the Chaplain of the Royal Cornwall Infirmary, who later became Curate at Newquay.

One Tippett who left his home in Cornwall to seek fame and fortune elsewhere was Henry William Tippett. Born in 1858, he became a lawyer, land investor and owner of a hotel in the south of France. He married Isabel Clementina Binny Kemp in London in 1903. She was a qualified nurse and also a novelist, playwright, pacifist and Suffragette, imprisoned for a short time for her activities. Isabel was also a cousin to Charlotte Despard, British-born, Irish-based Suffragette and Sinn Fein activist. Henry and Isabel's first son was born in 1904, named Peter Kemp Tippett. He later had a successful naval career but it is their second son, Michael Kemp Tippett, who was to become more famous.

Prep school for him was followed by an uncomfortable two year spell in Fettes College, a public school in Edinburgh, before he moved south to attend Stamford Grammar School in Lincolnshire, where he continued his love of playing piano under the guidance of Mrs Frances Tinkler, who also named Malcolm Sargent as one of her former pupils. Michael Tippett wanted more than anything to become a composer and worked towards this end despite many setbacks. By 1930 he had progressed sufficiently to be giving concerts featuring music he had written himself or adapted from the works of other composers. The teaching of music provided him an income sufficient to continue composing through the 1930s and by 1941, he had completed his first major work, an oratorio entitled 'A Child of our Time'. He became a conscientious objector during the Second World War and this led to a short term of imprisonment when he refused to perform even non-combat military work in 1943. After the war he made frequent broadcasts on radio and his popularity led to him being given the task of composing a 'Suite for the Birth of Prince Charles', commissioned by the BBC and performed under the baton of Sir Adrian Boult. Another royal piece, 'Garland for the Queen', was composed for the coronation of Queen Elizabeth in 1952. Music for strings, piano, orchestra and voice were all in his range and he became one of England's best known twentieth-century composers. He died on 8 January 1998 at the age of ninety-three.

TRE...

There are so many Cornish family names beginning with this prefix, indeed probably enough to fill a whole book on their own, that it is difficult to choose just a sample for inclusion here. The prefix means 'homestead', 'farm' or even 'village', and Cornwall has at least as many 'Tre-'prefixed place names as it does saints names. The sample I have chosen is picked out purely on numerical frequency within our datum point of the 1861 census. It does not therefore include Trelawny, with or without the 'e' before the 'y'. Cornish, historical, the stuff of legend, but sadly by 1861 there are but a small handful left in Cornwall. Neither do Trefry or Treffry feature, equally ancient and also famous, but in small numbers. Trerise, and many others fall way short of making the top of the list in pure numbers, and so please excuse their omission.

TREBILCOCK

A name where the prefix is as above, 'homestead' or 'farm', but where the meaning of the suffix is subject to some debate. Some sources consider that the true meaning is lost in the mists of time, whilst others suggest it is from *Tre Pyl Cok*, meaning 'house on the hill of the cuckoo'. Again I have no desire to come down on one side or the other. It is found across Cornwall, but is most prevalent in mid-Cornwall, particularly around the parishes of St Columb Minor and St Columb Major and their neighbours.

Trebilcock as a place name is to be found a little further east in the parish of Roche. Documents confirming ownership of this place by Sir Richard Edgcumbe can still be found dating from as far back as 1624. Even before this, the name appears as Trebiloc, dating from the early fourteenth century. The true meaning, like the cuckoo, may be quite elusive but it is certainly a Cornish name going back many centuries.

TREGONING

From *Tre Ke Onnen,* meaning 'house' or 'homestead' with an 'ash tree hedge' or 'boundary', this name is found with one 'n' or a double 'n' in the middle, and also with other variants such as Tregonen. Again, it is an ancient name and again, it is also found as a place name. Perhaps the most significant of the several Tregonning place names in Cornwall is Tregonning Hill, which straddles the parishes of Breage and Germoe just west of Helston. It was here in 1746 that a Devonshire man, William Cookworthy, first found commercial quantities of china clay. He was visiting the nearby Great Work mine, one of Cornwall's best known tin mines, and noticed that the men were using a type of clay they called Moorstone to repair furnaces. Cookworthy took some samples and found that the clay was excellent for making porcelain, and he was soon leaseholder of several workings on Tregonning Hill. Because of the presence of mica in these deposits, the quality of this clay was not as good as that later exploited in the St Austell area and as a result, Cornwall's main china clay industry moved further east, where it still remains today as a major employer.

Archaeological work at Tregonning Hill suggests human habitation going back to the sixth century and records from the fourteenth century show a name here of Tregonan. Another possible explanation of the name as 'Conan's farm' lies in this spelling. The Helston and Penzance area have a majority of Tregonings in Victorian census records, with Redruth close behind. Many, as might be expected from the locations, are miners and as such the name has spread far and wide like many other Cornish names in the past couple of hundred years.

Thomas Henry Tregonning, originally from Gwennap, was one such miner who went with his family to the Cornish stronghold of Galena, Jo Daviess County, Illinois. The family are later to be found in Clear Creek, Colorado, and their story is one which ended in tragic violence. Life in these mining towns was harsh, especially in the winter months when the weather was far worse than anything which the Cornish miners had ever experienced at home. The local newspapers were full of reports of fighting and violence and on 22 January 1873, they reported that Thomas Henry Tregonning, known to all as Harry, had murdered his wife. He tried to kill himself as well but succeeded only in breaking his arm with the shot. He was eventually found and imprisoned but before he could stand trial he escaped with the help of his brother and the two of them headed north towards Canada. Whether they made it or not is the subject of some speculation, but their story proves that life for our emigrating miners did not always turn out to be perfect, as promised by the agents who went around local villages and towns painting a rosy picture of fortunes to be made, better living conditions and far better prospects than Cornwall had to offer.

Another Thomas Tregoning to make a name for himself in a totally different way in America is described by one biographer as, 'a self made man who, without family or pecuniary advantages at the commencement of his life, has battled earnestly and energetically and by indomitable courage and integrity has achieved success and gained a comfortable competence.' High praise indeed.

This second Thomas Tregoning was born not far from the first. His father, also Thomas, was a mine captain and the family lived at Tuckingmill. When he was in his early twenties he went to Columbia to be deputy manager of a silver mine. He returned to Cornwall about three years later and worked for a while in mining here in the employ of the

Bolitho family of Penzance before emigrating to America in 1869. Here he held a variety of mining positions in iron ore mines before turning his attention to the real estate business. This, together with his agencies for a host of insurance companies, saw him become a prominent citizen of Evans, Colorado, by the 1890s. The name might be the same, indeed the two men were born within a few miles of each other, but the tide of fame and fortune favoured them in totally different ways.

TRELOAR

This name is derived from *Tre,* meaning 'home' or 'homestead', and *Lowarth,* meaning 'garden', so a name for those who live in a house with a garden. As with many other names we have looked at, the name of Treloar is almost 100 per cent found in Cornwall or borne by those who are of direct Cornish origin. Over half of Cornwall's Treloar families are to be found in the Helston area where many are miners in and around Wendron parish. The name here is a very ancient one and has been found as far back as 1333 under its original spelling of Trelowarth, both as a family name and a place name, proof if ever it were needed that family names often come from their place of abode. Wendron parish registers are preserved from as early as 1562 and some of the earliest references to the name of Trelowarth to be found there are of a marriage for Robert Trelowarth to Alice John in 1574 and of baptisms of their children, including Wearne Trelowarth. He was baptised in 1583 and sadly died at the age of two in 1585. Child mortality in Cornwall and elsewhere was high in those days and had not improved much by Victorian times, when we first find the name of William Purdie Treloar. He was born in London in 1843, the son of Thomas Treloar, who is described on later census data as a 'cocoa mat manufacturer', born in Portishead, Somerset. Although there is nothing Cornish about these birth places, the family line before them was Cornish through and through. William's mother, formerly Elizabeth Robertson, was originally from Pitlochry in Scotland.

　William left school at the age of fifteen and joined his father's business, later rising to become head of the company. His mother died in 1859 and his father remarried in 1861 to Isabel Purdie, a distant cousin from whose family William had inherited his middle name. Whilst his father moved away and spent his retirement on the Isle of Wight, William remained in London running the family business and becoming involved in politics. He was elected to the Court of Common Council for the ward of Farringdon Without, which spanned the area around Smithfield market and Chancery Lane. He was now in a position to expand his work with disabled and under-privileged children, of whom there were many in his local area. He was reelected unopposed to the council as the Children's Alderman in 1891. His political and public career continued to flourish and in 1906, he was elected Lord Mayor of London. During his term of office he raised over £60,000 for the Princess Louise Military Hospital and the newly formed Lord Mayor Treloar Cripple's Hospital and College. So popular and well received was his new venture that on 13 June 1907, he was able to write in his diary: 'Queen Alexandra came to Mansion House to open the Queen's Fete in aid of my Cripples Fund.' The main aim of his work with children was to ensure that those disadvantaged and sidelined because of illnesses such as tuberculosis could enjoy the fresh air and relative freedom of the countryside, away from the grime and smog of London which served only to worsen their medical condition. His facility, which also provided these children with an education, was located at Alton, Hampshire. A second branch at Hayling Island was opened in 1919. The Treloar Trust, Treloar School and Treloar College of Further Education are still to be found today at Alton and remain testaments to this man of Cornish stock who did so much to improve the impoverished lives of London's children.

TREMAYNE

Sometimes found as Tremaine, the *Tre* is again 'homestead', while the *Meyn* is 'stone'. It is said that if you are of the Tremayne spelling, then you are from the west of the county and if you are of the Tremaine spelling, you are from the east. This is true of two place names, Tremayne between Praze and Black Rock near Camborne in west Cornwall, whilst at the other end of Cornwall is Tremaine, one of the county's smallest rural parishes just west of Launceston. The '-yne' ending is found as a family name mainly around Falmouth and Helston and the '-aine' ending does appear around Camelford, but alas, both spellings occur around Redruth and Truro in the middle of the county and other Tremaine/Tremayne place names are also dotted around all over, so bang goes the theory that spelling and geography are linked.

What is certain is that the Tremayne family have made a name for themselves in various parts of the county. Lt Col. Arthur Tremayne, born in 1827, fought with the 13th Light Dragoons in the Crimean War, where he commanded Troop E at the Charge of the Light Brigade. He represented Truro as Member of Parliament from 1878 to 1880, and still found time to be an early patron of Cornish cricket at both the Mylor and Perranarworthal clubs. The family home was at Carclew in Mylor parish. His father was John Hearle Tremayne of Heligan and his mother was Caroline Lemon, daughter of Sir William and sister of Sir Charles, both of whom did so much to improve nineteenth-century Truro. The Tremayne name first came to Heligan as far back as the fifteenth century when the estate was in the hands of Sampson Tremayne. William Tremayne built himself a grand house there in 1603 and this was largely replaced in the early nineteenth century, around the same time as Henry Hawkins Tremayne was busy designing much of the grounds and grand gardens which have been restored in recent years. John Hearle Tremayne's son, John, married into the Glynn family of Bodmin. His daughter, Mary, married into the Boscawen family, whilst daughter Harriet married John Salusbury Salusbury-Trelawny, a direct descendant of Bishop Jonathan Trelawny, so famously imprisoned in the Tower of London and about whom every Cornish man and woman sings with such passion.

So all in all, it is quite a well-connected family name.

TREMBATH

A name derived from *Tre an Bagh,* 'house' or 'homestead' in the 'corner' or 'nook'. It is another name which is predominantly found in the far west of Cornwall with the parishes of Morvah, Sancreed and St Just having a fair proportion of the countywide Trembath families. Almost 85 per cent of Victorian Trembath families were living in or west of Penzance or had immediate family connections to that area. Parish registers in this area are available from as early as any in Cornwall and these show the name goes back over 400 years. Earlier than that there is mention of Andre Trenybah in ancient Madron documents and an indenture dated 1442 which gives the name of Richard Trembagh Wartha. There is also a Crows Trembagh or Trembath Cross listed among the ancient crosses of Cornwall. The whereabouts of this cross today are unclear, with only a small stump remaining in its original location.

TRENOWETH

—///—

Sometimes given as Trenowth, the suffix means 'new', so we have 'folk who live in the new house'. It is yet another name which is predominantly found in west Cornwall and one which, for some reason, appears to have been changed to Ternouth in many east Cornwall records. Probably the 'throaty' pronunciation of the prefix has fooled many a census enumerator or scribe of parish registers and other documents down the years. It is a way in which names evolve and are changed as we have seen with others.

Like many Cornish names, the name of Trenoweth is now to be found all over the world. One family who left their native Cornwall for Australia was the family of William and Phyllis Trenoweth of St Buryan. William Trenoweth, or Trenouth as it is given in some records, was born in 1802, son of another William and his wife, Elizabeth. The family were of farming stock. William junior married Phyllis Hutchins on 15 April 1826 in St Buryan Church, and the census of 1841 shows the family at Tregadgwith, St Buryan, with five children; John, Eliza, Prudence, William and Samuel. By the census of 1851 the family are to be found at Trewoofe, St Buryan, with children Prudence, Amelia and Rosetta. The sons are living in and working on farms in the locality, typical of a Cornish farming family of the time. Things were to change when on 15 December 1854, William, Phyllis and children William, Samuel, Amelia and Rosetta set sail aboard the *Lady MacDonald* bound from Plymouth to Port Adelaide in Australia. Listed on board are 'Mr & Mrs Santo and seven children in the cabin and 283 Government Emigrants in the Steerage.' Many are listed as being selected by the company agent, Mr Woolcock and are from various parts of Cornwall and other West Country locations. A few are listed as being 'aided by the Highland and Island Society of

Scotland selected by Reverend Otto Trevelyan from among his own parishioners'.

Like Cornwall, Scotland and other parts of Britain were suffering hardship and depression and many families were finding new lives on the other side of the world. The journey to Australia was as tough and arduous as any one of the hundreds which sailed at this time of mass emigration. Five births are recorded on the voyage and seven deaths, two of these occurring in the few days in which the ship was 'laying off', a period where ships were anchored just offshore from their destination to undergo medical and other checks before the passengers were allowed ashore. The Trenoweth family finally set foot on Australian soil on 14 April 1855. Work was plentiful, as this was a time when new mineral reserves in southern Australia were being discovered and exploited. Farmers such as the Trenoweth family had no difficulty obtaining land and growing crops to feed the hungry mining communities and others. The family thrived and grew, the children eventually becoming parents and grandparents, with Trenoweth descendants still to be found today in their newly adopted land.

Another, more tragic family story comes in the shape of Nancy Trenoweth and is told by William Bottrell, who we have met before, in his book, *Hearthside Stories of West Cornwall*. The story, entitled 'Nancy Trenoweth, the Fair Daughter of the Miller of Alsia', is a classic tale of true love thwarted by parental disapproval and a perceived class difference. Nancy was the daughter of a miller from Lower Alsia in St Buryan parish whose lands included productive orchards and was 'as pleasant a spot as any in Buryan'. Her lover on the other hand was a farmer's son, Frank Lanyon, who with his father, Hugh, scratched a living from the highlands at nearby Bosean.

The two families were distantly related and Nancy was sent to work for the Lanyon family and, needless to say, young love blossomed between her and Frank. Parental disapproval soon intervened and tried to split the lovers but they still managed, in the best traditions of any Romeo and Juliet, many clandestine meetings in the dead of night. The consequences were inevitable. William Bottrell puts it in such a superb way when he says:

> The ancient dames of the hamlet easily divined from the cherished remembrance of the experience of their own youthful days, what would be the result of the nightly meetings of the impulsive and thoughtless

Above and overleaf: Alsia Mill, near St Buryan, parts of which have been dated to the thirteenth century, was the home of Nancy Trenoweth. Her tragic tale is told by William Bottrell in his book *Hearthside Stories of West Cornwall*.

young lovers. Before the winter passed, the wise dames' forebodings proved but too true.

To cut a long story short, Nancy was with child and Frank was the father. Still the families fought and tried to keep the lovers apart. Frank went off to sea with others of the parish, swearing true love for eternity. The tale ends, again almost inevitably, in tragic shipwreck and loss of life, with poor Frank one of the unfortunate victims. Before his soul could rest, he sprang up, a ghostly form on horseback and seized his true love, riding off into the full mooned night only to be parted again by fate. So stricken was she with grief that she took to her bed the following day and passed peacefully away. Her body was laid beside his, together for eternity.

TRESIDDER

A name where the largest concentrations are in the Falmouth and Helston areas, the suffix here is generally considered to be derived from the personal name *Seder*, so 'Seder's farm' or 'homestead'. It is a name where some of its bearers have not always been honest and

upright citizens. A letter dated 15 September 1768 from the Customs
Officer at Penzance to his superiors in Bristol reads:

> In consequence of ye honours orders of 17th June, we had caused to
> be arrested three of the people concerned in running wool to France.
> Richard Tresidder, Rich. Tresidder the younger and Thos. Tresidder, all
> sent to be secured in the Sheriff's ward for want of proper security. John
> Tresidder and Richard Richards not yet taken.

1771 sees these same four Tresidder names again on charges of
smuggling wool. The excise men did not have it all their own way
though, as a subsequent report states: 'I fear a criminal prosecution
would be useless at best, for a reason it shocks me to mention, that a
Cornish jury would certainly acquit the smugglers.' Fair trade they
called it.

Other Tresidder names are also to be found in the Quarter Sessions
Court records. In 1814, Elizabeth Tresidder of Budock was fined 1s for
'keeping a common bawdy house and an ill governed and disorderly
house.' Later the same year, this same Elizabeth Tresidder was fined for
assault.

In 1821, John Tresidder, described as an 'oil manufacturer' was
fined for assaulting Samuel Downing whilst Robert Tresidder, 'gent
of Constantine', was also fined for assault. In 1836, James Tresidder of
Ludgvan was given 'six months hard labour and a private whipping'
for stealing a quantity of ribbon, workboxes and 100 combs. But not
all have been of bad character. Many were good honest mining folk,
working hard to earn a living for their families.

We have already met an Antarctic glacier and a Rocky Mountain
township named after Cornishmen, and the name of Tresidder offers
us another geographical feature of note in Tresidder Peak, 3,231 metres
high in the Cathedral Range in California's Yosemite National Park.
It is named after Donald Bertram Tresidder, who was president of
the Yosemite Park from 1925 to 1948 and also President of Stanford
University from 1943 to 1948. I have not been able to positively
confirm his Cornish connections, but there is a tantalising possibility
that his grandfather was a Cornish miner who went to America from
this part of the world.

TRETHEWEY

Homestead of *Dewi,* David to you and me, this is a name which is found predominantly in central Cornwall's china clay district with the parishes of St Stephen and St Dennis being the heartland of the name. As might be expected, many are employed in the china clay industry which has been a major employer in this area for over 250 years. As we have noted under the Tregonning name, china clay in the St Austell area was found to be purer than the original Cornish deposits found to the west of Helston.

Among the Trethewey families in the St Stephen area in 1861 is William, his wife, Martha, and son, Jabez, born in 1851 and the youngest of four children of the family. Jabez did not follow other family members into the china clay industry, instead he trained as a carpenter, a skill very much in demand when he emigrated to New Zealand in the 1870s. He married Mary Wallace, a Cornish girl, and in 1892 the couple had a son and named him William Thomas, after his grandfather. William left his schooling at the age of thirteen and followed his father into the woodworking profession, concentrating on carving such things as ornate fire surrounds and headboards for beds. He soon moved on and extended his wood carving talents under the guidance of Frederick Gurnsey, a sculptor of some note in Christchurch. William was mainly self-taught, studying the human anatomy and the works of such greats as Rodin and Michelangelo. He made the change from wood to stone with ease and was commissioned to carve many statues and memorials, including a war memorial to New Zealand's fallen of the First World War in Kaiapoi. The detail of this soldier, even down to a broken boot lace, is quite remarkable. It is carved from one five ton piece of Italian marble and stands 10ft high. The memorial set William Trethewey at the top of his profession, and later commissions included work on the Christchurch Civic Theatre and on the ornate façade of a Christchurch shopping arcade, as well as statues and busts of the great and the good of New Zealand. In 1928 he won a competition for what is perhaps his best known work, a statue of Captain James Cook. Carved from twelve tons of Italian marble and set atop a solid granite base, the statue stands proudly some 20ft from base to the brim of his hat and depicts Cook with one hand resting on a ship's capstan and his telescope in the other, gazing out over the gardens of Victoria Square, Christchurch, as he would have gazed over the vast expanses of the undiscovered far reaches of the Pacific Ocean on his voyages of discovery.

Although William Thomas Trethewey was never a miner or a china clay worker, he suffered ill health in his later years caused by breathing in dust from the stone he carved, reminiscent of the dreaded 'Miner's Lung' of his Cornish homeland. He died in Christchurch on 4 May 1956.

TREVENA

The suffix here is one where at least two different interpretations have been found. It could be from *Veneth,* meaning 'hill' or *Vun,* meaning 'minerals', and there is also a school of thought suggesting it is one and the same name as the Spanish *Trevino* and comes from a part of northern Spain bearing that name. This is quite possible given that trade between Cornwall and Spain and the whole of the area down the eastern seaboard of the Atlantic as far as the Mediterranean has been ongoing for a couple of millennia at least. Again it is not a name which would ever make the top of the list in terms of sheer numbers, but its occurrence at least up to mid-Victorian times outside Cornwall is rare. Since then, like so many of the names we have seen, it has spread worldwide.

John Henry Trevena, son of William and Mary from Gwennap, went to America where he became a respected teacher and preacher in Tennessee. Canadian-born Ernest Henham may not at first seem to have any connection to Cornish Trevena families, but his family were originally from these parts and he spent most of his life living on Dartmoor and writing novels based there under the pen name of John Trevena. American author Samuel Trevena Jackson got his middle name from his Cornish ancestry, and pottery by Henry Trevena is much prized in Australia.

So many different names in such far off places, all from Cornish roots.

TREVITHICK

This is another name where the place name has given rise to the family name. *Budic* or *Vudic* seems to be the origin of the second part, so we have 'homestead of Budic'. Some of the oldest references to the place name relate to Trevithick Manor on the southern outskirts of Newquay. One early reference to this place name in 1648 is in the marriage settlement of Elizabeth, daughter of Thomas Arundell of St Columb, to Richard Bluet, gentleman of Colan. There are several other Trevithick place names across Cornwall, but the name will always be most closely associated with Richard Trevithick, inventor, engineer and probably the best known and most written about Cornishman ever.

He was born in 1771 in Illogan to a father who was senior mine captain at the great Dolcoath mine and a mother whose family name of Teague was also one with generations of mining experience. A later marriage into the Harvey family of Hayle, famed worldwide for their revolutionary mine engines, boilers and other great mining machinery, added another notch to his mining and engineering pedigree.

Little wonder then that Richard Trevithick was destined to a career in mine related industries. But it was not as an ordinary miner or even mine captain that he made his name. From an early age he showed much promise in his quick learning and understanding. As a result he set about solving some of the problems encountered in the mining industry and his greatest ally in this was his harnessing of the power of steam. With this he invented steam powered engines which were the first ever to run on roads, 'Goin' up Camborne Hill comin' Down', at Christmas 1801. This was closely followed in 1804 by his pioneer steam engine running on rails in a Welsh coalfield, with an improved display model in London in 1808. He travelled the world over the next twenty years from the north of England to Peru in South America, pioneering steam traction and power. Sadly his gift for invention was not matched by a gift for patenting or making money from his work, or receiving the full public credit due to him, and history has chosen in many cases to remember the name of Stephenson, father and son, rather than Trevithick as the first steam pioneers.

As a family name it is another found mainly in the west of Cornwall, with few Trevithick names to be found east of Redruth. But what of others, perhaps for generations overshadowed by their famous namesake?

The Trevithick name crops up, as you would expect, in mining communities all over the world. Henry Trevithick, for example, born in Sithney in 1811, married Elizabeth Pascoe there in 1836 and by the late 1840s the family are found in the Burra mining area of Australia. Here, Henry worked in the mines, and he, Elizabeth and as many as eleven children are found in records there with a stated place of abode as 'a tent close to the police camp'. Tented communities or other primitive dwellings hewn out of the river banks, along which these early pioneers moved looking for gold, were the main early housing in the Burra area.

Henry later moved his family 300 miles or so south to the Ballarat area of Victoria and here opened two hotels, The Locomotive and The Commercial in the Avoca Township. The first of these was aptly named, having an owner by the name of Trevithick. This was another of the great mining areas of southern Australia where many Cornish families are to be found. Henry did quite well in the hotel business and he also speculated in mining ventures, but with mixed results. On one occasion he is reported to be 'lighting his pipe with five pound notes', such was his success, but other reports tell that his long term rewards from mining were quite poor. He became a member of the local council and a worthy citizen of the area. This was all despite an incident in 1859 when he and a close friend, Henry Knott, had a beer tent at the local racecourse one day. It seems that the two Henrys may both have been the worse for drink by the end of the day, perhaps as a result of their winnings, perhaps merely through sampling their own ales, we may never know. But on the way home the wagon being driven at considerable speed by Henry Trevithick hit a rut in the road, spilling the unfortunate Henry Knott. He landed on his head and by all accounts was killed instantly. At the inquest Henry Trevithick maintained that he was sober and that it was only the deceased who was drunk, but witnesses suggested that both men were 'well over the limit', shall we say. No further charges were brought against Henry Trevithick as a result of the accident, but it could have been much worse had the inquest considered he was to blame and brought charges similar to 'causing death whilst under the influence of drink'.

Henry Knott had been an influential and wealthy citizen of the town and was buried in the new cemetery at Avoca. By some strange quirk of fate it was he who had only recently given this parcel of land to the community as a graveyard, and his was one of the first burials to take place there. To add even more insult to injury, his poor widow had to pay £20 to the local council to bury her husband in a plot given by his own benevolence.

Henry Trevithick lived on well into his seventies and died in 1887, newspaper reports of the time giving his cause of death as 'a general break-up of the bodily system.'

TYACK

I have mentioned before that this name and Teague have, in the past, been confused and interchanged, but most sources agree that they are distinct in their origins with Teague coming from *Tek* or 'fair', whereas Tyack is from *Tyak,* meaning 'peasant' or 'farmer'. There are very few Tyack families east of Truro and indeed the Truro area has almost half of the county's population of the name. Many of these are tin and copper miners in St Agnes, Kea and Kenwyn parishes. The name is also to be found in the village of Devoran, with some records having an 'e' tagged on to the end. John Frederick Tyacke was a long standing member of the Feock Parish Council in the early years of the twentieth century. He was an accountant by profession and later became superintendent of the Redruth and Chacewater Railway, the mineral line which ran from the heartland of the mining district around Redruth down to the port of Devoran on the south coast, from where ore was exported and many cargoes associated with the mines like timber and coal were imported. There was also a Richard Tyacke, shoemaker of that same village of Devoran for many years. Like many of the names we have met, Tyack is now to be found far and wide across mining areas of the world.

UREN

There are about 750 Uren names on the 1861 census of England and Wales, of which about 650 are living in Cornwall. Of the others, most are living in other areas traditionally associated with mining. Some are just over the Tamar in the Tavistock area, whilst others are to be found in

Wales, Durham and Northumberland. Of those in Cornwall over 44 per cent are in the Penzance area and another 35 per cent are in the Redruth area. The Uren families of the Penzance area are mostly in and around Lelant and St Ives, and occupations include mining, farming, fishing and other trades associated with the sea. Of parishes a little further east, Gwinear, Wendron, Illogan and Gwennap have their fair share of Uren families and most have employment in the mining industry.

Surviving parish registers of baptism, marriage and burial show the Uren name under a variety of spellings, as is expected of these oldest registers, as far back as the 1564 marriage of Thomas Urine and Elizabeth, no surname given, in St Mawgan in Pydar. 1574 in Breage has Otes Uren marrying Elizabeth Cornall, and 1580 in the same parish gives a burial of Elane Uren. The spelling interpretation of Uryn appears in several entries in the early 1600s in Breage, but gradually down the years the spelling has been standardised to its present form.

Mining Uren families are to be found all over the world and there is a tiny dot on the map of Mexico near Guadalajara named Uren after one of its founding fathers, a Cornish miner.

VARCOE

This is another name of uncertain origins and another to be concentrated in quite a small area. Most Varcoe or Vercoe families are to be found in the St Austell area, from the south coast around the Roseland Peninsula, Mevagissey and St Ewe to parishes further inland around St Dennis and others of the Cornish china clay area.

In the parish of St Just in Roseland, several Varcoe families are to be found in eighteenth and early nineteenth-century records, and the name here dates back at least a couple of centuries before this time. One of these families is that of Philip Varcoe and his wife, Jane, formerly Odgers, who were married in Falmouth in 1801. They settled in St Mawes, where Philip was in the building trade and among their children were Philip, baptised on 30 October 1803 in St Just in Roseland Parish Curch, and Bryant, also baptised in St Just in Roseland on 23 October 1809. Philip junior followed in his father's footsteps in the building trade and became a mason, and Bryant went into farming. Both sons later married, Philip to Catherine Collins on 21 June 1825, and Bryant on 23 October 1837, in the same beautifully situated church right down by the river in St Just in Roseland. His bride was Elizabeth Tiddy, another family name with very long associations with this part of Cornwall.

By the census of 1841, both families are to be found in St Just parish. Philip Varco, as it is spelt here, is living in St Mawes with his wife, Catherine, and children; Samuel, aged ten, Philip, nine, Elizabeth, eight, Martha, six, John, four, Arthur, two, and the baby William, just seven months. Not far away at Polvarth, St Just, is Bryant Vercoe, with wife Elisabeth, their son James, aged one and Catherine Vercoe, at aged fourteen a daughter of his brother Philip. This is one of the last records of this family here in Cornwall for on 2 November 1841 the Varcoe family were aboard the *Timandra* bound from Plymouth, England to New Plymouth, New Zealand, one of the first ever migrant ships to make the voyage.

Among the cabin passengers are the names of William Devenish from Dorset and Josiah Flight, who brought with them ten ewes and two rams, the first sheep to arrive in New Zealand. Among the 200 or so steerage passengers are Philip and Catherine Vercoe, as it is spelt, with Mary Jane, aged sixteen, shown as a seamstress who was living in St Mawes with her grandmother at the time of the 1841 census, plus their other children, Catherine, Samuel, Philip, Elizabeth, Martha, John, Arthur and William. As well as this branch of the family, Bryant and his wife Elizabeth and two year old son James were also aboard, as was Martha, a younger sister who had left her job as a dressmaker in Truro to join the family on passage to the other side of the world. Their voyage was tinged with sadness and with joy. Two year old James died a month into the voyage and was buried at sea on 6 December 1841. In all, five young children and a girl of seventeen died at sea, all before arriving for a two week break in the voyage in Cape Town over the Christmas period. Some accounts suggest the high death rate so early in the journey was due to the lack of experience of the ship's captain, Captain Skinner, but the account of the ship's doctor, Dr George Forbes, perhaps gives some clues. He says, 'There is a quiet cabin (referring to the dozen or so paying passengers in cabin class) and in the steerage a little Ireland or hell of swearing, filth, theft and pilfering'. He quickly drew up a new set of rules for the steerage passengers on matters relating to health, hygiene and general day-to-day living, and this seems to have had some effect, but still he reports that some 'do nothing from morn 'til night but make puddings, compositions of bacon and fat, eat and cook, eternally eating and cooking…'. He adds, 'there are some good men, at present eclipsed, the Brookings, Harrison, Allan, Treweek, Clare, Vercoes and Prout.' Not everyone on these migrant ships were good honest workers seeking a better life like the Varcoe brothers and their families.

By the time the *Timandra* reached New Plymouth, five infants had been born on the voyage, one of them a daughter named Catherine to Bryant and Elizabeth Varcoe.

The Varcoe families soon settled into their lives in New Plymouth, already a town of some 500 inhabitants when they arrived. The men easily found work, and by 1845 their eldest daughter, Mary Jane, had married another migrant, Hannibal Marks. The following year Philip, second son of Philip and Catherine, married Ann Foreman, daughter of a family from Kent who were migrants to New Zealand even earlier than the Varcoe families. Generation followed generation and today there are large numbers of New Zealanders who can trace their ancestry back to these early migrant journeys, many of them to the Varcoe family from St Mawes and St Just in Roseland. There is also a Timandra Motel on Timandra Street, New Plymouth, named after the ship which brought the Varcoe families to their new homeland.

VIVIAN

As with Tremain and Tremayne you are either a Vivian or a Vyvyan, and both are equally ancient names here in Cornwall, dating back many centuries. The Vyvyan family of Trelowarren has a family archive of many volumes dating back as far as about 1240 which detail their estate holdings, marriage settlements, wills, and a huge variety of other material giving a full history of this wealthy Cornish family line. In the east of the county the family of Vivian of Glynn in Cardinham and others are also documented back several centuries, so it is a very old and very Cornish family name, many of whom down the centuries have been of great wealth, power and influence, both here in Cornwall and further afield.

As for the origin of the name, some say it is from the Latin *Vivianus* or *Vivus* meaning 'alive' or 'lively'. Others suggest that it came across with a fifth-century French saint or even, once again, with William the Conqueror. The version I prefer is that it is derived from the Celtic

word for 'flee' or 'escape' and that the origins of the family lie in the
lost land of Lyonesse. Family legend will tell you that a Vyvyan was the
last Lord of Lyonesse and that he escaped on a white horse as his once
great land sank beneath the waves between Land's End and the Isles
of Scilly. He landed near St Buryan on the Cornish coast and many
long lost generations of the family held an estate there at Treviddren or
Trevederne, as it is sometimes spelt. Tales of the family being wreckers,
pirates and even murderers come down from this shady past.

In 1328 Richard Vyvyan of Treviddren and his two sons, William and
Hugh were, along with other St Buryan men, excommunicated by the
Church for assaulting Richard Beaupre, rector of St Just in Penwith,
whose duties included Canon of St Buryan. The assault had actually
taken place in the churchyard at St Buryan and was seen as an act
violating all Christian morals and values. The family later settled down
and became respectable enough for John Vyvyan to marry, in 1426, the
heiress of the Trelowarren estate, a holding which still extends to some
1,000 acres just south of the Helford River. This began a continuous
occupation of Trelowarren lands which has seen successive generations
provide many famous names here in Cornwall and nationally. The
family later married into the even more powerful Arundell family
of Trerice. Michael Vyvyan was the first Captain of St Mawes Castle
when it was built as part of Henry VIII's coastal defences. In 1642
Sir Richard Vyvyan, a noted Royalist, was given command of a new

Opposite and above: Godolphin House, Trelowarren, home of the Vyvyan family for well over 500 years.

fort at St Dennis Head at the entrance to the Helford River; he also bore the cost of its construction. The Baronetcy of Trelowarren was created in 1645 and Sir Richard Vyvyan, (1613-1665) became the 1st Baronet, the honour being bestowed by King Charles himself at Boconnoc. Richard's wife, the former Mary Bulteel of Barnstaple in Devon, was at this time Lady in Waiting to Queen Henrietta Maria, wife of the king. Richard Vyvyan's contribution to Cornish life also included his duties at various times as MP for Penryn, Tregony and St Mawes and he held the office of Master of the Mint.

Sir Vyell Vyvyan (1639-1697), 2nd Baronet, was MP for St Mawes and Helston and 3rd Baronet, Sir Richard Vyvyan (1676-1724), was MP for Mitchell and a prominent Jacobite. Down the line we find further members of Parliament, high-ranking army officers, churchmen and a philosopher in the 8th Baronet, the fourth to bear the name Sir Richard Vyvyan, who was born in 1800. He was educated at Harrow and Christ Church, Oxford, but left there before graduating as he inherited the estate in 1820, rather sooner than expected on the death of his father, and the work of running the estate and keeping up with his many other interests left him no time to complete his studies. He also seems to have found no time to marry, such was his hectic lifestyle. He became a Fellow of the Royal Society in 1826, wrote on scientific subjects, with a particular interest in physics, penned a novel but never had it published, and also kept an unpublished diary, written in Italian. The work which took up most of his time was a lengthy parliamentary career, during which he represented a variety of seats from Cornwall through to Okehampton in Devon and as far as Bristol; anywhere it seems which was easy to win at the time when 'rotten boroughs' were still in fashion, or anywhere which would accept his often radical views. He was extremely passionate on many issues, so much so that he was often well out of step with his fellow Tories. After a brief retirement from politics from 1837 to 1840 he became MP for Helston from 1841 to 1857 before retiring gracefully to Trelowarren.

He was often to be seen in later years riding the estate and the surrounding area on his white horse. Part of the Vyvyan legend about the family escape from the doomed land of Lyonesse was that the one surviving Vyvyan rode a white horse to the safety of the Cornish shore, and from that day onwards a white horse was always kept in harness and in readiness, should the need ever arise for the Vyvyan family to flee its lands again. Sir Richard Carew of Antony in his 1602 *Survey of Cornwall* notes that, 'the Vyvyans anciently bore argent, a lion rampant, gules, standing on the waves of the sea (which waves have of late been left out) and still give for their crest a horse, argent, on which they tell you the governor escaped.' The white horse of Lyonesse lives on.

In comparison, the history of the Vivian family of Glynn may not seem quite so glamorous but in their very different way they have been equally as important and influential down many centuries. Their history goes back well over 500 years. The family are recorded in the St Columb area in the reign of Henry VII, well before 1500, and the last Prior of Bodmin was of the Vivian family before its closure in the 1530s. Very early in their history the Vivian family married into the Glynn family and began their occupation of Glynn lands just to the east of Bodmin, in what we now know as the Glynn Valley. It was much later in the seventeenth and eighteenth centuries that the family came to even greater prominence.

John Vivian of Truro became Vice Warden of the Stannaries and is affectionately remembered as 'the father of the Cornish copper trade.' In 1785 he joined with Francis Basset of Tehidy in forming the Cornish Metal Company, and over the following few years they began to buy up all the copper mined in Cornwall. His interests then extended to South Wales where he set up copper smelting works, fired by the abundance of Welsh coal. His son, John Henry (1785-1855), stayed in Swansea building up this business, and in turn his son, Henry Hussey Vivian (1821-1894), set Swansea up to be known as the metallurgical centre of the world. He represented Truro and several Welsh seats as MP and was made Lord Swansea in 1893. All of this was despite action being taken against his smelting works for an excess of pollution which caused the total abandonment of several farms in the Hafod area of Swansea. Jobs, it seems, were of more importance than the pollution they caused and the owners of even the worst polluting factories and smelting works were almost above the law, provided they kept on employing local workers and bringing prosperity to the area. Thankfully, different criteria operate today.

Richard Hussey Vivian, brother to John Henry, had a distinguished army career, rising to the rank of Lieutenant General at a time when rank and rapid promotion could be bought with family wealth rather than earned on the field of battle. He became the first Baron Vivian, spent two years in France just to learn the language and married into the long established French Huguenot family of Philip Champion de Crespigny, who had escaped to England in 1585 following the Edict of Fontainebleau by which Louis XIV banned their religious beliefs and set about destroying their churches. Richard Hussey Vivian hangs today in all his military splendour among the great and the good in the National Portrait Gallery in London.

The Glynn family house in the Glynn Valley is not as old as some of the landed gentry's country seats in other parts of Cornwall. The original mansion was taken down, those parts at least which had not fallen down, and rebuilt in the Georgian style. Sadly, that lasted only a short time before being destroyed by fire in 1791. Its rebuilding was under the supervision of Richard Hussey Vivian, when he was not off learning French or campaigning with the army. The estate was handed down through other generations of the family until the 1940s when ever increasing expenses forced its sale. It lay almost forgotten for a further twenty years but happily enjoyed a renaissance under the new ownership of Dr Peter Mitchell, a biochemist and Nobel Prize winner who bought the estate in 1962. He renovated the house and it became the headquarters of the Glynn Research Foundation in 1974, a new lease of life for an ageing building with so many stories to tell of its generations of famous occupants.

CONCLUSION

We have now come to the end of our look at over 100 of the most common names of Cornish origin to be found in the county in the mid-nineteenth century. Doubtless there will be those whose inclusion or omission will cause discussion and query. No study of this sort will ever find all the answers or, in one short volume, be able to do adequate justice to every name of Cornish, Celtic or any other origin. It is but a selection and one I hope which has triggered some interest and a desire to find out more. If so, the object of the exercise has been fulfilled.

As we said in our introduction, to err is human, and inescapable.